THE ONE
IN RED CRAVAT

A COLLECTION
OF POEMS IN ODE TO
THE ROBIN REDBREAST

By

VARIOUS

WITH AN INTRODUCTORY ESSAY
BY JOHN BURROUGHS

Read & Co.

CONTENTS

4

BIRDS AND POETS

An Essay by John Burroughs

It might almost be said that the birds are all birds of the poets and of no one else, because it is only the poetical temperament that fully responds to them. So true is this, that all the great ornithologists—original namers and biographers of the birds— have been poets in deed if not in word. Audubon is a notable case in point, who, if he had not the tongue or the pen of the poet, certainly had the eye and ear and heart—"the fluid and attaching character"—and the singleness of purpose, the enthusiasm, the unworldliness, the love, that characterize the true and divine race of bards.

So had Wilson, though perhaps not in as large a measure; yet he took fire as only a poet can. While making a journey on foot to Philadelphia, shortly after landing in this country, he caught sight of the red-headed woodpecker flitting among the trees,—a bird that shows like a tricolored scarf among the foliage,—and it so kindled his enthusiasm that his life was devoted to the pursuit of the birds from that day. It was a lucky hit. Wilson had already set up as a poet in Scotland, and was still fermenting when the bird met his eye and suggested to his soul a new outlet for its enthusiasm.

The very idea of a bird is a symbol and a suggestion to the poet. A bird seems to be at the top of the scale, so vehement and intense is his life,—large-brained, large-lunged, hot, ecstatic, his frame charged with buoyancy and his heart with song. The beautiful vagabonds, endowed with every grace, masters of all climes, and knowing no bounds,—how many human

9

aspirations are realized in their free, holiday lives, and how many suggestions to the poet in their flight and song!

Indeed, is not the bird the original type and teacher of the poet, and do we not demand of the human lark or thrush that he "shake out his carols" in the same free and spontaneous manner as his winged prototype? Kingsley has shown how surely the old minnesingers and early ballad-writers have learned of the birds, taking their key-note from the blackbird, or the wood-lark, or the throstle, and giving utterance to a melody as simple and unstudied. Such things as the following were surely caught from the fields or the woods:—

> "She sat down below a thorn,
> Fine flowers in the valley,
> And there has she her sweet babe borne,
> And the green leaves they grow rarely."

Or the best lyric pieces, how like they are to certain bird-songs!—clear, ringing, ecstatic, and suggesting that challenge and triumph which the outpouring of the male bird contains. (Is not the genuine singing, lyrical quality essentially masculine?) Keats and Shelley, perhaps more notably than any other English poets, have the bird organization and the piercing wild-bird cry. This, of course, is not saying that they are the greatest poets, but that they have preëminently the sharp semi-tones of the sparrows and the larks.

But when the general reader thinks of the birds of the poets, he very naturally calls to mind the renowned birds, the lark and the nightingale, Old World melodists, embalmed in Old World poetry, but occasionally appearing on these shores, transported in the verse of some callow singer.

The very oldest poets, the towering antique bards, seem to make little mention of the song-birds. They loved better the soaring, swooping birds of prey, the eagle, the ominous birds, the vultures, the storks and cranes, or the clamorous sea-birds and the screaming hawks. These suited better the rugged, warlike character of the times and the simple, powerful souls of the singers themselves. Homer must have heard the twittering of the swallows, the cry of the plover, the voice of the turtle, and the warble of the nightingale; but they were not adequate symbols to express what he felt or to adorn his theme. Aeschylus saw in the eagle "the dog of Jove," and his verse cuts like a sword with such a conception.

It is not because the old bards were less as poets, but that they were more as men. To strong, susceptible characters, the music of nature is not confined to sweet sounds. The defiant scream of the hawk circling aloft, the wild whinny of the loon, the whooping of the crane, the booming of the bittern, the vulpine bark of the eagle, the loud trumpeting of the migratory geese sounding down out of the midnight sky; or by the seashore, the coast of New Jersey or Long Island, the wild crooning of the flocks of gulls, repeated, continued by the hour, swirling sharp and shrill, rising and falling like the wind in a storm, as they circle above the beach or dip to the dash of the waves,—are much more welcome in certain moods than any and all mere bird-melodies, in keeping as they are with the shaggy and untamed features of ocean and woods, and suggesting something like the Richard Wagner music in the ornithological orchestra.

> "Nor these alone whose notes
> Nice-fingered art must emulate in vain,
> But cawing rooks, and kites that swim sublime
> In still repeated circles, screaming loud,
> The jay, the pie, and even the boding owl,
> That hails the rising moon, have charms for me,"

says Cowper. "I never hear," says Burns in one of his letters, "the loud, solitary whistle of the curlew in a summer noon, or the wild mixing cadence of a troop of gray plovers in an autumnal morning, without feeling an elevation of soul like the enthusiasm of devotion or poetry."

Even the Greek minor poets, the swarm of them that are represented in the Greek Anthology, rarely make affectionate mention of the birds, except perhaps Sappho, whom Ben Jonson makes speak of the nightingale as—

"The dear glad angel of the spring."

The cicada, the locust, and the grasshopper are often referred to, but rarely by name any of the common birds. That Greek grasshopper must have been a wonderful creature. He was a sacred object in Greece, and is spoken of by the poets as a charming songster. What we would say of birds the Greek said of this favorite insect. When Socrates and Phaedrus came to the fountain shaded by the plane-tree, where they had their famous discourse, Socrates said: "Observe the freshness of the spot, how charming and very delightful it is, and how summer-like and shrill it sounds from the choir of grasshoppers." One of the poets in the Anthology finds a grasshopper struggling in a spider's web, which he releases with the words:—

"Go safe and free with your sweet voice of song."

Another one makes the insect say to a rustic who had captured him:—

"Me, the Nymphs' wayside minstrel whose sweet note
O'er sultry hill is heard, and shady grove to float."

Still another sings how a grasshopper took the place of a broken string on his lyre, and "filled the cadence due."

"For while six chords beneath my fingers cried,
He with his tuneful voice the seventh supplied;
The midday songster of the mountain set
His pastoral ditty to my canzonet;
And when he sang, his modulated throat
Accorded with the lifeless string I smote."

While we are trying to introduce the lark in this country, why not try this Pindaric grasshopper also?

It is to the literary poets and to the minstrels of a softer age that we must look for special mention of the song-birds and for poetical rhapsodies upon them. The nightingale is the most general favorite, and nearly all the more noted English poets have sung her praises. To the melancholy poet she is melancholy, and to the cheerful she is cheerful. Shakespeare in one of his sonnets speaks of her song as mournful, while Martial calls her the "most garrulous" of birds. Milton sang:—

"Sweet bird, that shunn'st the noise of folly,
Most musical, most melancholy,
Thee, chantress, oft the woods among
I woo, to hear thy evening song."

To Wordsworth she told another story:—

"O nightingale! thou surely art
A creature of ebullient heart;
These notes of thine,—they pierce and pierce,—
Tumultuous harmony and fierce!
Thou sing'st as if the god of wine
Had helped thee to a valentine;
A song in mockery and despite
Of shades, and dews, and silent night,
And steady bliss, and all the loves
Now sleeping in these peaceful groves."

13

In a like vein Coleridge sang:—

> "'T is the merry nightingale
> That crowds and hurries and precipitates
> With fast, thick warble his delicious notes."

Keats's poem on the nightingale is doubtless more in the spirit of the bird's strain than any other. It is less a description of the song and more the song itself. Hood called the nightingale

> "The sweet and plaintive Sappho of the dell."

I mention the nightingale only to point my remarks upon its American rival, the famous mockingbird of the Southern States, which is also a nightingale,—a night-singer,—and which no doubt excels the Old World bird in the variety and compass of its powers. The two birds belong to totally distinct families, there being no American species which answers to the European nightingale, as there are that answer to the robin, the cuckoo, the blackbird, and numerous others. Philomel has the color, manners, and habits of a thrush,—our hermit thrush,—but it is not a thrush at all, but a warbler. I gather from the books that its song is protracted and full rather than melodious,—a capricious, long-continued warble, doubling and redoubling, rising and falling, issuing from the groves and the great gardens, and associated in the minds of the poets with love and moonlight and the privacy of sequestered walks. All our sympathies and attractions are with the bird, and we do not forget that Arabia and Persia are there back of its song.

Our nightingale has mainly the reputation of the caged bird, and is famed mostly for its powers of mimicry, which are truly wonderful, enabling the bird to exactly reproduce and even improve upon the notes of almost any other songster. But in a state of freedom it has a song of its own which is infinitely rich and various. It is a garrulous polyglot when it chooses to be, and

14

there is a dash of the clown and the buffoon in its nature which too often flavors its whole performance, especially in captivity; but in its native haunts, and when its love-passion is upon it, the serious and even grand side of its character comes out.

In Alabama and Florida its song may be heard all through the sultry summer night, at times low and plaintive, then full and strong.

A friend of Thoreau and a careful observer, who has resided in Florida, tells me that this bird is a much more marvelous singer than it has the credit of being. He describes a habit it has of singing on the wing on moonlight nights, that would be worth going South to hear. Starting from a low bush, it mounts in the air and continues its flight apparently to an altitude of several hundred feet, remaining on the wing a number of minutes, and pouring out its song with the utmost clearness and abandon,—a slowly rising musical rocket that fills the night air with harmonious sounds. Here are both the lark and nightingale in one; and if poets were as plentiful down South as they are in New England, we should have heard of this song long ago, and had it celebrated in appropriate verse. But so far only one Southern poet, Wilde, has accredited the bird this song. This he has done in the following admirable sonnet:—

TO THE MOCKINGBIRD

Winged mimic of the woods! thou motley fool!
  Who shall thy gay buffoonery describe?
Thine ever-ready notes of ridicule
  Pursue thy fellows still with jest and gibe.
Wit—sophist—songster—Yorick of thy tribe,
  Thou sportive satirist of Nature's school,
To thee the palm of scoffing we ascribe,
  Arch scoffer, and mad Abbot of Misrule!
For such thou art by day—but all night long
  Thou pour'st a soft, sweet, pensive, solemn strain,

As if thou didst in this, thy moonlight song,
   Like to the melancholy Jaques, complain,
Musing on falsehood, violence, and wrong,
   And sighing for thy motley coat again.

Aside from this sonnet, the mockingbird has got into poetical literature, so far as I know, in only one notable instance, and that in the page of a poet where we would least expect to find him,—a bard who habitually bends his ear only to the musical surge and rhythmus of total nature, and is as little wont to turn aside for any special beauties or points as the most austere of the ancient masters. I refer to Walt Whitman's "Out of the cradle endlessly rocking," in which the mockingbird plays a part. The poet's treatment of the bird is entirely ideal and eminently characteristic. That is to say, it is altogether poetical and not at all ornithological; yet it contains a rendering or free translation of a bird-song—the nocturne of the mockingbird, singing and calling through the night for its lost mate—that I consider quite unmatched in our literature:—

Once, Paumanok,
When the snows had melted, and the Fifth-
month grass was growing,
Up this seashore, in some briers,
Two guests from Alabama—two together,
And their nest, and four light green eggs, spotted with brown,
And every day the he-bird, to and fro, near at hand,
And every day the she-bird, crouched on her nest, silent,
with bright eyes,
And every day I, a curious boy, never too close, never
disturbing them,
Cautiously peering, absorbing, translating.

Shine! Shine! Shine!
Pour down your warmth, great Sun!
While we bask—we two together.

Two together!
Winds blow South, or winds blow North,
Day come white, or night come black,
Home, or rivers and mountains from home,
Singing all time, minding no time,
If we two but keep together.

Till of a sudden,
Maybe killed unknown to her mate,
One forenoon the she-bird crouched not on the nest,
Nor returned that afternoon, nor the next,
Nor ever appeared again.

And thenceforward all summer, in the sound of the sea,
And at night, under the full of the moon, in calmer weather,
Over the hoarse surging of the sea,
Or flitting from brier to brier by day,
I saw, I heard at intervals, the remaining one, the he-bird,
The solitary guest from Alabama.

Blow! blow! blow!
Blow up, sea-winds, along Paumanok's shore!
I wait and I wait, till you blow my mate to me.

Yes, when the stars glistened,
All night long, on the prong of a moss-scalloped stake,
Down, almost amid the slapping waves,
Sat the lone singer, wonderful, causing tears.

He called on his mate:
He poured forth the meanings which I, of all men, know.

Soothe! soothe! soothe!
Close on its wave soothes the wave behind,
And again another behind, embracing and lapping,
every one close,
But my love soothes not me, not me.

Low hangs the moon—it rose late.
Oh it is lagging—oh I think it is heavy with love, with love.

Oh madly the sea pushes, pushes upon the land,
With love—with love.

O night! do I not see my love fluttering
out there among the breakers!
What is that little black thing I see there in the white?

Loud! loud! loud!
Loud I call to you, my love!
High and clear I shoot my voice over the waves:
Surely you must know who is here, is here;
You must know who I am, my love.

Low-hanging moon!
What is that dusky spot in your brown yellow?
Oh it is the shape, the shape of my mate!
O moon, do not keep her from me any longer.

Land! land! O land!
Whichever way I turn, oh I think you could give
my mate back again, if you only would;
For I am almost sure I see her dimly whichever way I look.

O rising stars!
Perhaps the one I want so much will rise, will rise with some
of you.

O throat! O trembling throat!
Sound clearer through the atmosphere!
Pierce the woods, the earth;
Somewhere listening to catch you, must be the one I want.

Shake out, carols!
Solitary here—the night's carols!
Carols of lonesome love! Death's carols!
Carols under that lagging, yellow, waning moon!
Oh, under that moon, where she droops almost down into
the sea!
O reckless, despairing carols.

But soft! sink low! Soft! let me just murmur;
And do you wait a moment, you husky-noised sea;
For somewhere I believe I heard my mate responding to me,
So faint—I must be still, be still to listen!
But not altogether still, for then she might
not come immediately to me.

Hither, my love!
Here I am! Here!
With this just-sustained note I announce myself to you;
This gentle call is for you, my love, for you.

Do not be decoyed elsewhere!
That is the whistle of the wind—it is not my voice;
That is the fluttering, the fluttering of the spray;
Those are the shadows of leaves.

O darkness! Oh in vain!
Oh I am very sick and sorrowful.

The bird that occupies the second place to the nightingale in British poetical literature is the skylark, a pastoral bird as the Philomel is an arboreal,—a creature of light and air and motion, the companion of the plowman, the shepherd, the harvester,— whose nest is in the stubble and whose tryst is in the clouds. Its life affords that kind of contrast which the imagination loves,— one moment a plain pedestrian bird, hardly distinguishable from the ground, the next a soaring, untiring songster, reveling in the upper air, challenging the eye to follow him and the ear to separate his notes.

The lark's song is not especially melodious, but is blithesome, sibilant, and unceasing. Its type is the grass, where the bird makes its home, abounding, multitudinous, the notes nearly all alike and all in the same key, but rapid, swarming, prodigal, showering down as thick and fast as drops of rain in a summer shower.

Many noted poets have sung the praises of the lark, or been kindled by his example. Shelley's ode and Wordsworth's "To a Skylark" are well known to all readers of poetry, while every schoolboy will recall Hogg's poem, beginning:—

"Bird of the wilderness,
  Blithesome and cumberless,
Sweet be thy matin o'er moorland and lea!
  Emblem of happiness,
  Blest is thy dwelling-place—
Oh to abide in the desert with thee!"

I heard of an enthusiastic American who went about English fields hunting a lark with Shelley's poem in his hand, thinking no doubt to use it as a kind of guide-book to the intricacies and harmonies of the song.

He reported not having heard any larks, though I have little doubt they were soaring and singing about him all the time, though of course they did not sing to his ear the song that Shelley heard.

The poets are the best natural historians, only you must know how to read them. They translate the facts largely and freely.

A celebrated lady once said to Turner, "I confess I cannot see in nature what you do." "Ah, madam," said the complacent artist, "don't you wish you could!"

Shelley's poem is perhaps better known, and has a higher reputation among literary folk, than Wordsworth's; it is more lyrical and lark-like; but it is needlessly long, though no longer than the lark's song itself, but the lark can't help it, and Shelley can. I quote only a few stanzas:—

> "In the golden lightning
>   Of the sunken sun,
> O'er which clouds are bright'ning
>   Thou dost float and run,
> Like an unbodied joy whose race is just begun.
>
> "The pale purple even
>   Melts around thy flight;
> Like a star of heaven,
>   In the broad daylight
> Thou art unseen, but yet I hear thy shrill delight,
>
> "Keen as are the arrows
>   Of that silver sphere,
> Whose intense lamp narrows
>   In the white dawn clear,
> Until we hardly see—we feel that it is there;

"All the earth and air
    With thy voice is loud,
As, when Night is bare,
    From one lonely cloud
The moon rains out her beams, and Heaven is overflowed."

Wordsworth has written two poems upon the lark, in one of which he calls the bird "pilgrim of the sky." This is the one quoted by Emerson in "Parnassus." Here is the concluding stanza:—

"Leave to the nightingale her shady wood;
A privacy of glorious light is thine,
Whence thou dost pour upon the world a flood
Of harmony, with instinct more divine;
Type of the wise, who soar, but never roam,
True to the kindred points of heaven and home."

The other poem I give entire:—

"Up with me! up with me into the clouds!
    For thy song, Lark, is strong;
Up with me, up with me into the clouds!
    Singing, singing,
With clouds and sky about thee ringing,
    Lift me, guide me till I find
That spot which seems so to thy mind!

"I have walked through wilderness dreary,
    And to-day my heart is weary;
Had I now the wings of a Faery
    Up to thee would I fly.
There is madness about thee, and joy divine
    In that song of thine;
Lift me, guide me high and high
To thy banqueting-place in the sky.

22

"Joyous as morning
Thou art laughing and scorning;
Thou hast a nest for thy love and thy rest,
And, though little troubled with sloth,
Drunken Lark! thou wouldst be loth
To be such a traveler as I.
    Happy, happy Liver!
With a soul as strong as a mountain river,
Pouring out praise to the Almighty Giver,
Joy and jollity be with us both!

"Alas! my journey, rugged and uneven,
Through prickly moors or dusty ways must wind;
But hearing thee, or others of thy kind,
As full of gladness and as free of heaven,
I, with my fate contented, will plod on,
And hope for higher raptures, when life's day is done."

But better than either—better and more than a hundred pages—is Shakespeare's simple line,—

"Hark, hark, the lark at heaven's gate sings,"

or John Lyly's, his contemporary,—

"Who is't now we hear?
None but the lark so shrill and clear;
Now at heaven's gate she claps her wings,
The morn not waking till she sings."

We have no well-known pastoral bird in the Eastern States that answers to the skylark. The American pipit or titlark and the shore lark, both birds of the far north, and seen in the States only in fall and winter, are said to sing on the wing in a similar strain. Common enough in our woods are two birds that have many of the habits and manners of the lark—the water-thrush and the golden-crowned thrush, or oven-bird. They are both walkers, and the latter frequently sings on the wing up aloft after the manner of the lark. Starting from its low perch, it rises in a spiral flight far above the tallest trees, and breaks out in a clear, ringing, ecstatic song, sweeter and more richly modulated than the skylark's, but brief, ceasing almost before you have noticed it; whereas the skylark goes singing away after you have forgotten him and returned to him half a dozen times.

But on the Great Plains, of the West there; is a bird whose song resembles the skylark's quite closely and is said to be not at all inferior. This is Sprague's pipit, sometimes called the Missouri skylark, an excelsior songster, which from far up in the transparent blue rains down its notes for many minutes together. It is, no doubt, destined to figure in the future poetical literature of the West.

Throughout the northern and eastern parts of the Union the lark would find a dangerous rival in the bobolink, a bird that has no European prototype, and no near relatives anywhere, standing quite alone, unique, and, in the qualities of hilarity and musical tintinnabulation, with a song unequaled. He has already a secure place in general literature, having been laureated by no less a poet than Bryant, and invested with a lasting human charm in the sunny page of Irving, and is the only one of our songsters, I believe, that the mockingbird cannot parody or imitate. He affords the most marked example of exuberant pride, and a glad, rollicking, holiday spirit, that can be seen among our birds. Every note expresses complacency and glee. He is a beau of the first pattern, and, unlike any other bird of my acquaintance, pushes his gallantry to the point of wheeling gayly into the train of every female that comes along, even after the season of courtship is over and the matches are all settled; and when she leads him on too wild a chase, he turns, lightly about and breaks out with a song is precisely analogous to a burst of gay and self-satisfied laughter, as much as to say, *"Ha!*

ha! ha! I must have my fun, Miss Silverthimble, thimble, thimble,
if I break every heart in the meadow, see, see, see!"

At the approach of the breeding season the bobolink undergoes a complete change; his form changes, his color changes, his flight changes. From mottled brown or brindle he becomes black and white, earning, in some localities, the shocking name of "skunk bird;" his small, compact form becomes broad and conspicuous, and his ordinary flight is laid aside for a mincing, affected gait, in which he seems to use only the very tips of his wings. It is very noticeable what a contrast he presents to his mate at this season, not only in color but in manners, she being as shy and retiring as he is forward and hilarious. Indeed, she seems disagreeably serious and indisposed to any fun or jollity, scurrying away at his approach, and apparently annoyed at every endearing word and look. It is surprising that all this parade of plumage and tinkling of cymbals should be gone through with and persisted in to please a creature so coldly indifferent as she really seems to be. If Robert O'Lincoln has been stimulated into acquiring this holiday uniform and this musical gift by the approbation of Mrs. Robert, as Darwin, with his sexual selection principle, would have us believe, then there must have been a time when the females of this tribe were not quite so chary of their favors as they are now. Indeed, I never knew a female bird of any kind that did not appear utterly indifferent to the charms of voice and plumage that the male birds are so fond of displaying. But I am inclined to believe that the males think only of themselves and of outshining each other, and not at all of the approbation of their mates, as, in an analogous case in a higher species, it is well known whom the females dress for, and whom they want to kill with envy!

I know of no other song-bird that expresses so much self-consciousness and vanity, and comes so near being an ornithological coxcomb. The red-bird, the yellowbird, the indigo-bird, the oriole, the cardinal grosbeak, and others, all birds of brilliant plumage and musical ability, seem quite unconscious of self, and neither by tone nor act challenge the admiration of the beholder.

By the time the bobolink reaches the Potomac, in September, he has degenerated into a game-bird that is slaughtered by tens of thousands in the marshes. I think the prospects now are of his gradual extermination, as gunners and sportsmen are clearly on the increase, while the limit of the bird's productivity in the North has no doubt been reached long ago. There are no more meadows to be added to his domain there, while he is being waylaid and cut off more and more on his return to the South. It is gourmand eat gourmand, until in half a century more I expect the blithest and merriest of our meadow songsters will have disappeared before the rapacity of human throats.

But the poets have had a shot at him in good time, and have preserved some of his traits. Bryant's poem on this subject does not compare with his lines "To a Water-Fowl,"—a subject so well suited to the peculiar, simple, and deliberate motion of his mind; at the same time it is fit that the poet who sings of "The Planting of the Apple-Tree" should render into words the song of "Robert of Lincoln." I subjoin a few stanzas:—

ROBERT OF LINCOLN

Merrily swinging on brier and weed,
  Near to the nest of his little dame,
Over the mountain-side or mead,
  Robert of Lincoln is telling his name:
      Bob-o'-link, bob-o'-link,
      Spink, spank, spink:
Snug and safe is that nest of ours,
Hidden among the summer flowers.
      Chee, chee, chee.

Robert of Lincoln is gayly drest,
  Wearing a bright black wedding-coat,
White are his shoulders and white his crest,
  Hear him call in his merry note:
        Bob-o'-link, bob-o'-link,
        Spink, spank, spink:
Look what a nice new coat is mine,
Sure there was never a bird so fine.
        Chee, chee, chee.

Robert of Lincoln's Quaker wife,
  Pretty and quiet, with plain brown wings,
Passing at home a patient life,
  Broods in the grass while her husband sings.
        Bob-o'-link, bob-o'-link,
        Spink, spank, spink:
Brood, kind creature; you need not fear
Thieves and robbers while I am here.
        Chee, chee, chee.

But it has been reserved for a practical ornithologist, Mr. Wilson Flagg, to write by far the best poem on the bobolink that I have yet seen. It is much more in the mood and spirit of the actual song than Bryant's poem:—

THE O'LINCOLN FAMILY

A flock of merry singing-birds were sporting in the grove;
Some were warbling cheerily, and some were making love:
There were Bobolincon, Wadolincon,
Winterseeble, Conquedle,—
A livelier set was never led by tabor, pipe, or fiddle,—
Crying, "Phew, shew, Wadolincon, see, see, Bobolincon,
Down among the tickletops, hiding in the buttercups!
I know the saucy chap, I see his shining cap
Bobbing in the clover there—see, see, see!"

Up flies Bobolincon, perching on an apple-tree,
Startled by his rival's song, quickened by his raillery.
Soon he spies the rogue afloat, curveting in the air,
And merrily he turns about, and warns him to beware!
"'T is you that would a-wooing go, down among the rushes O!
But wait a week, till flowers are cheery,—
wait a week,and, ere you marry,
Be sure of a house wherein to tarry!
Wadolink, Whiskodink, Tom Denny, wait, wait, wait!"

Every one's a funny fellow; every one's a little mellow;
Follow, follow, follow, follow, o'er the hill and in the hollow!
Merrily, merrily, there they hie; now they rise and now they fly;
They cross and turn, and in and out, and down
in the middle, and wheel about,—
With a "Phew, shew, Wadolincon! listen to me, Bobolincon!—
Happy's the wooing that's speedily doing, that's speedily doing,
That's merry and over with the bloom of the clover!
Bobolincon, Wadolincon, Winterseeble, follow, follow me!"

Many persons, I presume, have admired Wordsworth's poem
on the cuckoo, without recognizing its truthfulness, or how
thoroughly, in the main, the description applies to our own

species. If the poem had been written in New England or New York, it could not have suited our case better:—

"O blithe New-comer! I have heard,
   I hear thee and rejoice,
O Cuckoo! shall I call thee Bird,
   Or but a wandering Voice?

"While I am lying on the grass,
   Thy twofold shout I hear,
From hill to hill it seems to pass,
   At once far off, and near.

"Though babbling only to the Vale,
   Of sunshine and of flowers,
Thou bringest unto me a tale
   Of visionary hours.

"Thrice welcome, darling of the Spring!
   Even yet thou art to me
No bird, but an invisible thing,
   A voice, a mystery;

"The same whom in my schoolboy days
   I listened to; that Cry
Which made me look a thousand ways
   In bush, and tree, and sky.

"To seek thee did I often rove
   Through woods and on the green;
And thou wert still a hope, a love;
   Still longed for, never seen.

"And I can listen to thee yet;
  Can lie upon the plain
And listen, till I do beget
  That golden time again.

"O blesséd Bird! the earth we pace
  Again appears to be
An unsubstantial, faery place;
  That is fit home for thee!"

Logan's stanzas, "To the Cuckoo," have less merit both as poetry and natural history, but they are older, and doubtless the latter poet benefited by them. Burke admired them so much that, while on a visit to Edinburgh, he sought the author out to compliment him:—

"Hail, beauteous stranger of the grove!
  Thou messenger of spring!
Now Heaven repairs thy rural seat,
  And woods thy welcome sing.

"What time the daisy decks the green,
  Thy certain voice we hear;
Hast thou a star to guide thy path,
  Or mark the rolling year?

* * * * *

"The schoolboy, wandering through the wood
  To pull the primrose gay,
Starts, the new voice of spring to hear,
  And imitates thy lay.

* * * * *

30

"Sweet bird! thy bower is ever green,
  Thy sky is ever clear;
Thou hast no sorrow in thy song,
  No winter in thy year."

The European cuckoo is evidently a much gayer bird than ours, and much more noticeable.

"Hark, how the jolly cuckoos sing
'Cuckoo!' to welcome in the spring,"

says John Lyly three hundred years agone. Its note is easily imitated, and boys will render it so perfectly as to deceive any but the shrewdest ear. An English lady tells me its voice reminds one of children at play, and is full of gayety and happiness. It is a persistent songster, and keeps up its call from morning to night. Indeed, certain parts of Wordsworth's poem—those that refer to the bird as a mystery, a wandering, solitary voice—seem to fit our bird better than the European species. Our cuckoo is in fact a solitary wanderer, repeating its loud, guttural call in the depths of the forest, and well calculated to arrest the attention of a poet like Wordsworth, who was himself a kind of cuckoo, a solitary voice, syllabling the loneliness that broods over streams and woods,—

"And once far off, and near."

Our cuckoo is not a spring bird, being seldom seen or heard in the North before late in May. He is a great devourer of canker-worms, and, when these pests appear, he comes out of his forest seclusion and makes excursions through the orchards stealthily and quietly, regaling himself upon those pulpy, fuzzy titbits. His coat of deep cinnamon brown has a silky gloss and is very beautiful. His note or call is not musical but loud, and has in a remarkable degree the quality of remoteness and introvertedness.

It is like a vocal legend, and to the farmer bodes rain.

It is worthy of note, and illustrates some things said farther back, that birds not strictly denominated songsters, but criers like the cuckoo, have been quite as great favorites with the poets, and have received as affectionate treatment at their hands, as have the song-birds. One readily recalls Emerson's "Titmouse," Trowbridge's "Pewee," Celia Thaxter's "Sandpiper," and others of a like character.

It is also worthy of note that the owl appears to be a greater favorite with the poets than the proud, soaring hawk. The owl is doubtless the more human and picturesque bird; then he belongs to the night and its weird effects. Bird of the silent wing and expansive eye, grimalkin in feathers, feline, mousing, haunting ruins" and towers, and mocking the midnight stillness with thy uncanny cry! The owl is the great bugaboo of the feathered tribes. His appearance by day is hailed by shouts of alarm and derision from nearly every bird that flies, from crows down to sparrows. They swarm about him like flies, and literally mob him back into his dusky retreat. Silence is as the breath of his nostrils to him, and the uproar that greets him when he emerges into the open day seems to alarm and confuse him as it does the pickpocket when everybody cries Thief.

But the poets, I say, have not despised him:—

"The lark is but a bumpkin fowl;
    He sleeps in his nest till morn;
But my blessing upon the jolly owl
    That all night blows his horn."

Both Shakespeare and Tennyson have made songs about him. This is Shakespeare's, from "Love's Labor's Lost," and perhaps has reference to the white or snowy owl:—

"When icicles hang by the wall,
　And Dick the shepherd blows his nail,
And Tom bears logs into the hall,
　And milk comes frozen home in pail;
When blood is nipped and ways be foul,
Then nightly sings the staring owl,
　　　　Tu-whoo!
Tu-whit! tu-whoo! a merry note,
While greasy Joan doth keel the pot.

"When all aloud the wind doth blow,
　And coughing drowns the parson's saw,
And birds sit brooding in the snow,
　And Marian's nose looks red and raw;
When roasted crabs hiss in the bowl,
Then nightly sings the staring owl,
　　　　Tu-whoo!
Tu-whit! Tu-whoo! a merry note,
While greasy Joan doth keel the pot."

There is, perhaps, a slight reminiscence of this song in Tennyson's "Owl:"—

"When cats run home and light is come,
　And dew is cold upon the ground,
And the far-off stream is dumb,
　And the whirring sail goes round,
　And the whirring sail goes round;
　　Alone and warming his five wits,
　　The white owl in the belfry sits.

"When merry milkmaids click the latch,
    And rarely smells the new-mown hay,
And the cock hath sung beneath the thatch
    Twice or thrice his roundelay,
    Twice or thrice his roundelay;
        Alone and warming his five wits,
        The white owl in the belfry sits."

Tennyson has not directly celebrated any of the more famous birds, but his poems contain frequent allusions to them. The

"Wild bird, whose warble, liquid sweet,
    Rings Eden through the budded quicks,
    Oh, tell me where the senses mix,
Oh, tell me where the passions meet,"

of "In Memoriam," is doubtless the nightingale. And here we have the lark:—

"Now sings the woodland loud and long,
    And distance takes a lovelier hue,
    And drowned in yonder living blue
The lark becomes a sightless song."

And again in this from "A Dream of Fair Women:"—

"Then I heard
A noise of some one coming through the lawn,
And singing clearer than the crested bird
    That claps his wings at dawn."

The swallow is a favorite bird with Tennyson, and is frequently mentioned, beside being the principal figure in one of those charming love-songs in "The Princess."

His allusions to the birds, as to any other natural feature, show him to be a careful observer, as when he speaks of

"The swamp, where hums the dropping snipe."

His single bird-poem, aside from the song I have quoted, is "The Blackbird," the Old World prototype of our robin, as if our bird had doffed the aristocratic black for a more democratic suit on reaching these shores. In curious contrast to the color of its plumage is its beak, which is as yellow as a kernel of Indian corn. The following are the two middle stanzas of the poem:—

"Yet, though I spared thee all the spring,
    Thy sole delight is, sitting still,
    With that gold dagger of thy bill
To fret the summer jenneting.

"A golden bill! the silver tongue
    Cold February loved is dry;
    Plenty corrupts the melody
That made thee famous once, when young."

Shakespeare, in one of his songs, alludes to the blackbird as the ouzel-cock; indeed, he puts quite a flock of birds in this song:—

"The ouzel-cock so black of hue,
    With orange tawny bill;
The throstle with his note so true,
    The wren with little quill;
The finch, the sparrow, and the lark,
    The plain song cuckoo gray,
Whose note full many a man doth mark,
    And dares not answer nay."

So far as external appearances are concerned,—form, plumage, grace of manner,—no one ever had a less promising subject than had Trowbridge in the "Pewee." This bird, if not the plainest dressed, is the most unshapely in the woods. It is stiff and abrupt in its manners and sedentary in its habits, sitting around all day, in the dark recesses of the woods, on the dry twigs and branches, uttering now and then its plaintive cry, and "with many a flirt and flutter" snapping up its insect game.

The pewee belongs to quite a large family of birds, all of whom have strong family traits, and who are not the most peaceable and harmonious of the sylvan folk. They are pugnacious, harsh-voiced, angular in form and movement, with flexible tails and broad, flat, bristling beaks that stand to the face at the angle of a turn-up nose, and most of them wear a black cap pulled well down over their eyes. Their heads are large, neck and legs short, and elbows sharp. The wild Irishman of them all is the great crested flycatcher, a large, leather-colored or sandy-complexioned bird that prowls through the woods, uttering its harsh, uncanny note and waging fierce warfare upon its fellows. The exquisite of the family, and the braggart of the orchard, is the kingbird, a bully that loves to strip the feathers off its more timid neighbors such as the bluebird, that feeds on the stingless bees of the hive, the drones, and earns the reputation of great boldness by teasing large hawks, while it gives a wide berth to little ones.

The best beloved of them all is the phoebe-bird, one of the firstlings of the spring, of whom so many of our poets have made affectionate mention.

The wood pewee is the sweetest voiced, and, notwithstanding the ungracious things I have said of it and of its relations, merits to the full all Trowbridge's pleasant fancies. His poem is indeed a very careful study of the bird and its haunts, and is good poetry as well as good ornithology:—

"The listening Dryads hushed the woods;
   The boughs were thick, and thin and few
   The golden ribbons fluttering through;
Their sun-embroidered, leafy hoods
   The lindens lifted to the blue;
Only a little forest-brook
The farthest hem of silence shook;
When in the hollow shades I heard—
Was it a spirit or a bird?
Or, strayed from Eden, desolate,
Some Peri calling to her mate,
Whom nevermore her mate would cheer?
   'Pe-ri! pe-ri! peer!'

* * * * *

"To trace it in its green retreat
   I sought among the boughs in vain;
   And followed still the wandering strain,
So melancholy and so sweet,
   The dim-eyed violets yearned with pain.
'T was now a sorrow in the air,
Some nymph's immortalized despair
Haunting the woods and waterfalls;
And now, at long, sad intervals,
Sitting unseen in dusky shade,
His plaintive pipe some fairy played,
With long-drawn cadence thin and clear,—
   'Pe-wee! pe-wee! peer!'

"Long-drawn and clear its closes were—
  As if the hand of Music through
  The sombre robe of Silence drew
A thread of golden gossamer;
  So pure a flute the fairy blew.
Like beggared princes of the wood,
In silver rags the birches stood;
The hemlocks, lordly counselors,
Were dumb; the sturdy servitors,
In beechen jackets patched and gray,
Seemed waiting spellbound all the day
That low, entrancing note to hear,—
  'Pe-wee! pe-wee! peer!'

"I quit the search, and sat me down
  Beside the brook, irresolute,
  And watched a little bird in suit
Of sober olive, soft and brown,
  Perched in the maple branches, mute;
With greenish gold its vest was fringed,
Its tiny cap was ebon-tinged,
With ivory pale its wings were barred,
And its dark eyes were tender-starred.
"Dear bird," I said, "what is thy name?"
And thrice the mournful answer came,
So faint and far, and yet so near,—
  'Pe-wee! pe-wee! peer!'

"For so I found my forest bird,—
    The pewee of the loneliest woods,
    Sole singer in these solitudes,
Which never robin's whistle stirred,
    Where never bluebird's plume intrudes.
Quick darting through the dewy morn,
The redstart trilled his twittering horn
And vanished in thick boughs; at even,
Like liquid pearls fresh showered from heaven,
The high notes of the lone wood thrush
Fell on the forest's holy hush;
But thou all day complainest here,—
    'Pe-wee! pe-wee! peer!'"

Emerson's best natural history poem is the "Humble-Bee,"—a poem as good in its way as Burns's poem on the mouse; but his later poem, "The Titmouse," has many of the same qualities, and cannot fail to be acceptable to both poet and naturalist.

The chickadee is indeed a truly Emersonian bird, and the poet shows him to be both a hero and a philosopher. Hardy, active, social, a winter bird no less than a summer, a defier of both frost and heat, lover of the pine-tree, and diligent searcher after truth in the shape of eggs and larvae of insects, preëminently a New England bird, clad in black and ashen gray, with a note the most cheering and reassuring to be heard in our January woods,—I know of none other of our birds so well calculated to captivate the Emersonian muse.

Emerson himself is a northern hyperborean genius,—a winter bird with a clear, saucy, cheery call, and not a passionate summer songster. His lines have little melody to the ear, but they have the vigor and distinctness of all pure and compact things. They are like the needles of the pine—"the snow loving pine"—more than the emotional foliage of the deciduous trees, and the titmouse becomes them well:—

"Up and away for life! be fleet!—
The frost-king ties my fumbling feet,
Sings in my ears, my hands are stones,
Curdles the blood to the marble bones,
Tugs at the heart-strings, numbs the sense,
And hems in life with narrowing fence.
Well, in this broad bed lie and sleep,—
The punctual stars will vigil keep,—
Embalmed by purifying cold;
The wind shall sing their dead march old,
The snow is no ignoble shroud,
The moon thy mourner, and the cloud.

"Softly,—but this way fate was pointing,
'T was coming fast to such anointing,
When piped a tiny voice hard by,
Gay and polite, a cheerful cry,
Chick-chickadeedee! saucy note,
Out of sound heart and merry throat,
As if it said 'Good day, good sir!
Fine afternoon, old passenger!
Happy to meet you in these places,
Where January brings few faces.'

"This poet, though he lived apart,
Moved by his hospitable heart,
Sped, when I passed his sylvan fort,
To do the honors of his court,
As fits a feathered lord of land;
Flew near, with soft wing grazed my hands
Hopped on the bough, then darting low,
Prints his small impress on the snow,
Shows feats of his gymnastic play,
Head downward, clinging to the spray.

"Here was this atom in full breath,
Hurling defiance at vast death;
This scrap of valor just for play
Fronts the north-wind in waistcoat gray,
As if to shame my weak behavior;
I greeted loud my little savior,
'You pet! what dost here? and what for?
In these woods, thy small Labrador,
At this pinch, wee San Salvador!
What fire burns in that little chest,
So frolic, stout, and self-possest?
Henceforth I wear no stripe but thine;
Ashes and jet all hues outshine.
Why are not diamonds black and gray,
To ape thy dare-devil array?
And I affirm, the spacious North
Exists to draw thy virtue forth.
I think no virtue goes with size;
The reason of all cowardice
Is, that men are overgrown,
And, to be valiant, must come down
To the titmouse dimension.'

* * * * *

"I think old Caesar must have heard
In northern Gaul my dauntless bird,
And, echoed in some frosty wold,
Borrowed thy battle-numbers bold.
And I will write our annals new
And thank thee for a better clew.
I, who dreamed not when I came here
To find the antidote of fear,
Now hear thee say in Roman key,
Poean! Veni, vidi, vici."

A late bird-poem, and a good one of its kind, is Celia Thaxter's "Sandpiper," which recalls Bryant's "Water-Fowl" in its successful rendering of the spirit and atmosphere of the scene, and the distinctness with which the lone bird, flitting along the beach, is brought before the mind. It is a woman's or a feminine poem, as Bryant's is characteristically a man's.

The sentiment or feeling awakened by any of the aquatic fowls is preëminently one of loneliness. The wood duck which your approach starts from the pond or the marsh, the loon neighing down out of the April sky, the wild goose, the curlew, the stork, the bittern, the sandpiper, awaken quite a different train of emotions from those awakened by the land-birds. They all have clinging to them some reminiscence and suggestion of the sea. Their cries echo its wildness and desolation; their wings are the shape of its billows.

Of the sandpipers there are many varieties, found upon the coast and penetrating inland along the rivers and water-courses, one of the most interesting of the family, commonly called the "tip-up," going up all the mountain brooks and breeding in the sand along their banks; but the characteristics are the same in all, and the eye detects little difference except in size.

The walker on the beach sees it running or flitting before him, following up the breakers and picking up the aquatic insects left on the sands; and the trout-fisher along the farthest inland stream likewise intrudes upon its privacy. Flitting along from stone to stone seeking its food, the hind part of its body "teetering" up and down, its soft gray color blending it with the pebbles and the rocks, or else skimming up or down the stream on its long, convex wings, uttering its shrill cry, the sandpiper is not a bird of the sea merely; and Mrs. Thaxter's poem is as much for the dweller inland as for the dweller upon the coast:—

THE SANDPIPER

Across the narrow beach we flit,
  One little sandpiper and I;
And fast I gather, bit by bit,
  The scattered driftwood bleached and dry.
The wild waves reach their hands for it,
  The wild wind raves, the tide runs high,
As up and down the beach we flit,—
  One little sandpiper and I.

Above our heads the sullen clouds
  Scud black and swift across the sky;
Like silent ghosts in misty shrouds
  Stand out the white lighthouses high.
Almost as far as eye can reach
  I see the close-reefed vessels fly,
As fast we flit along the beach,—
  One little sandpiper and I.

I watch him as he skims along,
  Uttering his sweet and mournful cry;
He starts not at my fitful song,
  Or flash of fluttering drapery;
He has no thought of any wrong;
  He scans me with a fearless eye.
Stanch friends are we, well tried and strong,
  The little sandpiper and I.

Comrade, where wilt thou be to-night
  When the loosed storm breaks furiously?
My driftwood fire will burn so bright!
  To what warm shelter canst thou fly?
I do not fear for thee, though wroth
  The tempest rushes through the sky;

For are we not God's children both,
   Thou, little sandpiper, and I?

Others of our birds have been game for the poetic muse, but in most cases the poets have had some moral or pretty conceit to convey, and have not loved the bird first. Mr. Lathrop preaches a little in his pleasant poem, "The Sparrow," but he must some time have looked upon the bird with genuine emotion to have written the first two stanzas:—

"Glimmers gay the leafless thicket
   Close beside my garden gate,
Where, so light, from post to wicket,
   Hops the sparrow, blithe, sedate:
      Who, with meekly folded wing,
      Comes to sun himself and sing.

"It was there, perhaps, last year,
   That his little house he built;
For he seems to perk and peer,
   And to twitter, too, and tilt
      The bare branches in between,
      With a fond, familiar mien."

The bluebird has not been overlooked, and Halleek, Longfellow, and Mrs. Sigourney have written poems upon him, but from none of them does there fall that first note of his in early spring,—a note that may be called the violet of sound, and as welcome to the ear, heard above the cold, damp earth; as is its floral type to the eye a few weeks later Lowell's two lines come nearer the mark:—

"The bluebird, shifting his light load of song
From post to post along the cheerless fence."

44

Or the first swallow that comes twittering up the southern valley, laughing a gleeful, childish laugh, and awakening such memories in the heart, who has put him in a poem? So the hummingbird, too, escapes through the finest meshes of rhyme.

The most melodious of our songsters, the wood thrush and the hermit thrush,—birds whose strains, more than any others, express harmony and serenity,—have not yet, that I am aware, had reared to them their merited poetic monument, unless, indeed, Whitman has done this service for the hermit thrush in his "President Lincoln's Burial Hymn." Here the threnody is blent of three chords, the blossoming lilac, the evening star, and the hermit thrush, the latter playing the most prominent part throughout the composition. It is the exalting and spiritual utterance of the "solitary singer" that calms and consoles the poet when the powerful shock of the President's assassination comes upon him, and he flees from the stifling atmosphere and offensive lights and conversation of the house,—

"Forth to hiding, receiving night that talks not,
Down to the shores of the water, the path by the swamp in the dimness,
To the solemn shadowy cedars and ghostly pines so still."

Numerous others of our birds would seem to challenge attention by their calls and notes. There is the Maryland yellowthroat, for instance, standing in the door of his bushy tent, and calling out as you approach, *"which way, sir! which way, sir!"* If he says this to the ear of common folk, what would he not say to the poet? One of the peewees says *"stay there!"* with great emphasis. The cardinal grosbeak calls out *"what cheer" "what cheer;"* " the bluebird says *"purity," "purity," "purity;"* the brown thrasher, or ferruginous thrush, according to Thoreau, calls out to the farmer planting his corn, *"drop it," "drop it,"*

45

"cover it up," "cover it up" The yellow-breasted chat says *"who,"* *"who"* and *"tea-boy"* What the robin says, caroling that simple strain from the top of the tall maple, or the crow with his hardy haw-haw, or the pedestrain meadowlark sounding his piercing and long-drawn note in the spring meadows, the poets ought to be able to tell us. I only know the birds all have a language which is very expressive, and which is easily translatable into the human tongue.

AN ESSAY FROM
Birds and Poets, 1877

THE REDBREAST

By John Cotton

Sylvia Rubecula, Lath.

The Redbreast, or Robin, as he is occasionally denominated, is familiar with us from childhood. Before we can read we learn to repeat the fabled story of poor Cock Robin's death and burial. In all countries he is a favourite, and has what may be called a pet name. The inhabitants of Bornholm call him "Tommi-Liden;" the Norwegians, "Peter Ronsmed;" the Germans, "Thomas Gierdet;" and in England he is called by the more familiar appellation of "Bob." Wordsworth thus poetically addresses the Redbreast:—

> Art thou the bird whom man loves best,
> The pious bird with the scai'let breast,
>   Our little English Robin;
> The bird that comes about our doors
> When autumn winds are sobbing?
> Art thou the Peter of Norway boors?
>   Their Thomas in Finland
>   And Russia far inland?
> The bird who by some name or other
> All men who know thee call thee brother,
> The darling of children and men?—

The melodious notes of this little favourite are well known. Its song is sweet and well supported, and is continued almost throughout the year. During spring the Redbreast haunts the

47

wood, the grove, and the garden; it generally retires to thick hedgerows or other secluded spots to breed in, and is then seldom heard till autumn; when, on the retirement of our summer visitors, he again makes his appearance about our houses, and awakens our former attachment by pouring out his soft liquid carol, perched on some neighbouring shrub. It becomes the companion of the gardener, or faggot-maker in the woods, fluttering around and chirping its slender "pip." But when the cold grows more severe, and thick snow covers the ground, or frost hardens its surface, it approaches our houses, taps at the closed casement, casting sidelong glances indoors, as envious of the warm abode. It is probably attracted to the habitations of man by the shelter that it there obtains from the rigour of the weather, and in search of the insects that are collected in great numbers by the same cause.

The bill of the Redbreast is slender and delicate; its eyes are large, dark, and expressive, and its aspect mild. It is nearly six inches in length.

When wild, the Redbreast feeds on all sorts of insects, which are pursued with great skill and agility: sometimes, says Bechstein, this bird is seen fluttering like a butterfly round a leaf on which is a fly; or if he sees an earthworm, he hops forward, flapping his wings, and seizes it. In autumn he eats different sorts of berries.

In confinement, by giving him at first some earth or meal-worms, and in the autumn elderberries, he soon gets accustomed to eat anything: he picks up crumbs of bread, the little fibres of meat, and the like; but cheese appears his favourite food.[1]

The Redbreast is rather an unsociable bird with its own species, and drives away all others from his immediate neighbourhood. Obstinate battles are often maintained between the male birds.

The female builds her nest on the ground, at the roots of trees,

1 Bechstein's *Cage Birds*.

48

and in other concealed places. It is formed of the same materials as that of the Wren, but not so elaborately put together, and without a dome to the nest. If, however, there is not a natural concealment of foliage, the birds contrive to form an artificial one of dry leaves, under which they may reach the nest without the precise spot being known; and when the hen bird leaves her eggs, she sometimes covers them in the same manner; so that the strewing of leaves mentioned in the old ballad of the Babes in the Wood is true to the habits of the Redbreast. The eggs are yellowish grey, mottled with chestnut colour, and rarely exceed seven.[2]

Grahame has poetically sketched the habits of the Redbreast in the following lines:—

> High is his perch, but humble is his home,
> And well conceal'd; sometimes within the sound
> Of heartsome mill-clack, where the spacious door,
> White-dusted, tells him plenty reigns around—
> Close at the root of brier bush, that o'erhangs
> The narrow stream, with shealings bedded white,
> He fixes his abode, and lives at will.
> Oft near some single cottage he prefers
> To rear his little home; there, pert and spruce,
> He shares the refuse of the good-wife's churn.

As the evergreen shrubs are seen in their greatest beauty when other trees have lost their verdant hue, so the Redbreast assumes a gayer dress, and his song appears more sweet to us, when most other birds are mute, and our summer visitors have fled.

His melody is more generally heard when the arbutus, or strawberry-tree, is in all its beauty, exhibiting at once flowers and fruit; the blossoms of the present, with the ripe fruit of the former year.

---

2 Mudie's *British Birds.*

Spenser has illustrated the exuberance of this beautiful shrub in the following lines:—

> There is continual spring and harvest there
> Continual, both meeting at one time;
> For both the boughs do laughing blossoms bear,
> And with fresh colours deck the wanton prime,
> And eke at once the heavy trees they climb,
> Which seem to labour under their fruits load:
> The whiles the joyous birds make their pastime
> Amongst the shady leaves, their sweet abode,
> And their true loves without suspicion tell abroad.

A CHAPTER FROM
Song birds of Great Britain,
Part. 1, The resident Song Birds of Great Britain, 1858

THE ONE
IN RED CRAVAT

A COLLECTION
OF POEMS IN ODE TO
THE ROBIN REDBREAST

THE PETITION
OF THE RED-BREAST

By William Roscoe

AH! why did thy rude hand molest
The sacred quiet of my nest?
No more I rise on rapture's wing,
The ditties of my love to sing.
Restore me to the peaceful vale,
To wander with the southern gale;
Restore me to the woodland scene,
Romantic glen, or forest green;
To hail the Heaven's ethereal blue,
To drink the freshness of the dew;
Now, while my artless carols flow,
Let pity in thy bosom glow.
For this, at morn's inspiring hour,
I'll sing in thy luxuriant bow'r:
To thee the breeze of airy sigh
Shall waft my thrilling melody;
Thy soul the cadence wild shall meet,
The song of gratitude is sweet.
And at the pensive close of day,
When landscape-colours fade away,
Ah! then the robin's mellow note,
To thee in dying tone shall float; —
"Now, while my plaintive carols flow,

"Let pity in thy bosom glow;"
And I will consecrate to thee,
The wildest note of liberty.

EPITAPH ON A FREE BUT TAME REDBREAST

By William Cowper

A Favourite of Miss Sally Hurdis

THESE are not dew-drops, these are tears,
And tears by Sally shed
For absent Robin, who she fears,
With too much cause, is dead.

One morn he came not to her hand
As he was wont to come,
And, on her finger perched, to stand
Picking his breakfast-crumb.

Alarmed she called him, and perplext
She sought him, but in vain;
That day he came not, nor the next,
Nor ever came again.

She therefore raised him here a tomb,
Though where he fell, or how,
None knows, so secret was his doom,
Nor where he moulders now.

Had half a score of coxcombs died
In social Robin's stead,
Poor Sally's tears had soon been dried,
Or haply never shed.

But Bob was neither rudely bold
Nor spiritlessly tame,
Nor was, like theirs, his bosom cold,
But always in a flame.

INVITATION TO THE REDBREAST

———————————

By William Cowper

SWEET bird, whom the Winter constrains—
And seldom another it can—
To seek a retreat while he reigns,
In the well-sheltered dwellings of man,
Who never can seem to intrude,
Though in all places equally free,
Come! oft as the season is rude,
Thou art sure to be welcome to me.

At sight of the first feeble ray
That pierces the clouds of the east,
To inveigle thee every day
My windows shall show thee a feast;
For, taught by experience, I know
Thee mindful of benefit long,
And that, thankful for all I bestow,
Thou wilt pay me with many a song.

Then, soon as the swell of the buds
Bespeaks the renewal of Spring,
Fly hence, if thou wilt, to the woods,
Or where it shall please thee to sing:
And shouldst thou, compelled by a frost,
Come again to my window or door,
Doubt not an affectionate host,
Only pay, as thou payedst me before.

Thus music must needs be confest
To flow from a fountain above;
Else how should it work in the breast
Unchangeable friendship and love?
And who on the globe can be found,
Save your generation and ours,
That can be delighted by sound,
Or boasts any musical powers?

THE REDBREAST
CHASING THE BUTTERFLY

By William Wordsworth

Art thou the Bird whom Man loves best,
The pious Bird with the scarlet breast,
 Our little English Robin;
The Bird that comes about our doors
When Autumn winds are sobbing?
Art thou the Peter of Norway Boors?
 Their Thomas in Finland,
 And Russia far inland?
The Bird, whom by some name or other
All men who know thee call their Brother,
The Darling of Children and men?
Could[1] Father Adam open his eyes,
And see this sight beneath the skies,
He'd wish to close them again.

---

1 See *Paradise Lost, Book* XI, where Adam points out to Eve the
ominous sign of the Eagle chasing "two Birds of gayest plume,"
and the gentle Hart and Hind pursued by their enemy.

If the Butterfly knew but his friend,
Hither his flight he would bend;
And find his way to me
Under the branches of the tree:
In and out, he darts about;
Can this be the Bird, to man so good,
That, after their bewildering,
Did cover with leaves the little children,
    So painfully in the wood?

What ailed thee, Robin, that thou could'st pursue
    A beautiful Creature,
That is gentle by nature?
Beneath the summer sky
From flower to flower let him fly;
'Tis all that he wishes to do.
The Cheerer Thou of our in-door sadness,
He is the Friend of our summer gladness:
What hinders, then, that ye should be
Playmates in the sunny weather,
And fly about in the air together!
His beautiful wings in crimson are drest,
A crimson as bright as thine own:
If thou would'st be happy in thy nest,
O pious Bird! whom Man loves best,
Love him, or leave him alone!

AN EPITAPH ON A
ROBIN REDBEAST[2]

By Samuel Rogers

TREAD lightly here, for here, 'tis said,
When piping winds are hushed around,
A small note wakes from underground,
Where now his tiny bones are laid.
No more in lone and leafless groves,
With ruffled wing and faded breast,
His friendless, homeless spirit roves;
—Gone to the world where birds are blessed!
Where never cat glides o'er the green,
Or schoolboy's giant form is seen;
But Love, and Joy, and smiling Spring
Inspire their little souls to sing.

2 Inscribed on an urn in the flower-garden at Hafod.

ROBIN REDBREAST

By George Washington Doane

SWEET Robin, I have heard them say
That thou wert there upon the day
The Christ was crowned in cruel scorn
And bore away one bleeding thorn,—
That so the blush upon thy breast,
In shameful sorrow, was impressed;
And thence thy genial sympathy
With our redeemed humanity.

Sweet Robin, would that I might be
Bathed in my Saviour's blood, like thee;
Bear in my breast, whate'er the loss,
The bleeding blazon of the cross:
Live ever, with thy loving mind,
In fellowship with human kind;
And take my pattern still from thee,
In gentleness and constancy.

TO THE ROBIN

By Charles Tennyson Turner

The ox is all as happy in his stall
As when he lowed i' the Summer's yellow eve,
Browsing the king-cup slopes; but no reprieve
Is left for thee, save thy sweet madrigal,
Poor Robin! and severer days will fall.
Bethink thee well of all yon frosted sward,
The orchard-path so desolate and hard,
And meadow-runnels, with no voice at all!
Then feed with me, poor warbler, household bird,
And glad me with thy song so sadly timed,
And be on thankful ears thy lay conferr'd;
So, till her latest rhyme my muse hath rhymed,
Thy voice shall with a pleasant thrill be heard,
And with a poet's fear when twigs are lim'd.

THE REDBREAST (SUGGESTED IN A WESTMORELAND COTTAGE)

By William Wordsworth

Driven in by Autumn's sharpening air
From half-stripped woods and pastures bare,
Brisk Robin seeks a kindlier home:
Not like a beggar is he come,
But enters as a looked-for guest,
Confiding in his ruddy breast,
As if it were a natural shield
Charged with a blazon on the field,
Due to that good and pious deed
Of which we in the Ballad read.
But pensive fancies putting by,
And wild-wood sorrows, speedily
He plays the expert ventriloquist;
And, caught by glimpses now, now missed,
Puzzles the listener with a doubt
If the soft voice he throws about
Comes from within doors or without!
Was ever such a sweet confusion,
Sustained by delicate illusion?
He's at your elbow, to your feeling
The notes are from the floor or ceiling;
And there's a riddle to be guessed,
'Till you have marked his heaving chest,
And busy throat whose sink and swell,

Betray the Elf that loves to dwell
In Robin's bosom, as a chosen cell.

Heart-pleased we smile upon the Bird
If seen, and with like pleasure stirred
Commend him, when he's only heard.
But small and fugitive our gain
Compared with 'hers' who long hath lain,
With languid limbs and patient head
Reposing on a lone sick-bed;
Where now, she daily hears a strain
That cheats her of too busy cares,
Eases her pain, and helps her prayers.
And who but this dear Bird beguiled
The fever of that pale-faced Child;
Now cooling, with his passing wing,
Her forehead, like a breeze of Spring:
Recalling now, with descant soft
Shed round her pillow from aloft,
Sweet thoughts of angels hovering nigh,
And the invisible sympathy
Of "Matthew, Mark, and Luke, and John,
Blessing the bed she lies upon"?
And sometimes, just as listening ends
In slumber, with the cadence blends
A dream of that low-warbled hymn
Which old folk, fondly pleased to trim
Lamps of faith, now burning dim,
Say that the Cherubs carved in stone,
When clouds gave way at dead of night
And the ancient church was filled with light,
Used to sing in heavenly tone,
Above and round the sacred places
They guard, with winged baby-faces.

Thrice happy Creature! in all lands
Nurtured by hospitable hands:
Free entrance to this cot has he,
Entrance and exit both 'yet' free;
And, when the keen unruffled weather
That thus brings man and bird together,
Shall with its pleasantness be past,
And casement closed and door made fast,
To keep at bay the howling blast,
'He' needs not fear the season's rage,
For the whole house is Robin's cage.
Whether the bird flit here or there,
O'er table 'lilt', or perch on chair,
Though some may frown and make a stir,
To scare him as a trespasser,
And he belike will flinch or start,
Good friends he has to take his part;
One chiefly, who with voice and look
Pleads for him from the chimney-nook,
Where sits the Dame, and wears away
Her long and vacant holiday;
With images about her heart,
Reflected from the years gone by,
On human nature's second infancy.

THE AUTUMN ROBIN

By John Clare

Sweet little bird in russet coat,
  The livery of the closing year,
I love thy lonely plaintive note
  And tiny whispering song to hear,
While on the stile or garden seat
  I sit to watch the falling leaves,
The song thy little joys repeat
  My loneliness relieves.

And many are the lonely minds
  That hear, and welcome thee anew;
Not Taste alone, but humble hinds,
  Delight to praise, and love thee too.
The veriest clown, beside his cart,
  Turns from his song with many a smile,
To see thee from the hedgerow start,
  To sing upon the stile.

The shepherd on the fallen tree
  Drops down to listen to thy lay,
And chides his dog beside his knee,
  Who barks, and frightens thee away.
The hedger pauses, ere he knocks
  The stake down in the meadow-gap—
The boy, who every songster mocks,
  Forbears the gate to clap.

When in the hedge that hides the post
  Thy ruddy bosom he surveys,—
Pleased with thy song, in transport lost,
  He pausing mutters scraps of praise.
The maiden marks, at day's decline,
  Thee in the yard, on broken plough,
And stops her song, to listen thine,
  Milking the brindled cow.

Thy simple faith in man's esteem,
  From every heart hath favour won;
Dangers to thee no dangers seem—
  Thou seemest to court them more than shun.
The clown in winter takes his gun,
  The barn-door flocking birds to slay,
Yet should'st thou in the danger run
  He turns the tube away.

The gipsy boy, who seeks in glee
  Blackberries for a dainty meal,
Laughs loud on first beholding thee,
  When called, so near his presence steal.
He surely thinks thou know'st the call;
  And though his hunger ill can spare
The fruit, he will not pluck it all,
  But leaves some to thy share.

Upon the ditcher's spade thou'lt hop,
  For grubs and wreathing worms to search;
Where woodmen in the forest chop,
  Thou'lt fearless on their faggots perch;
Nay, by the gipsies' camp I stop,
  And mark thee dwell a moment there,
To prune thy wing awhile, then drop,
  The littered crumbs to share.

Domestic bird! thy pleasant face
    Doth well thy common suit commend;
To meet thee in a stranger-place
    Is meeting with an ancient friend.
I track the thicket's glooms around,
    And there, as loth to leave, again
Thou comest, as if thou knew the sound
    And loved the sight of men.

The loneliest wood that man can trace
    To thee a pleasant dwelling gives;
In every town and crowded place
    The sweet domestic robin lives.
Go where one will, in every spot
    Thy little welcome mates appear;
And, like the daisy's common lot,
    Thou'rt met with every where.

The swallow in the chimney tier,
    Or twittering martin in the eaves,
With half of love and half of fear
    His mortared dwelling shily weaves;
The sparrows in the thatch will shield;
    Yet they, as well as e'er they can,
Contrive with doubtful faith to build
    Beyond the reach of man.

But thou'rt less timid than the wren,
    Domestic and confiding bird!
And spots, the nearest haunts of men,
    Are oftenest for thy home preferred.
In garden-walls thou'lt build so low,
    Close where the bunch of fennel stands,
That e'en a child just taught to go
    May reach with tiny hands.

71

Sweet favoured bird! thy under-notes
 In summer's music grow unknown,
The concert from a thousand throats
 Leaves thee as if to pipe alone;
No listening ear the shepherd lends,
 The simple ploughman marks thee not,
And then by all thy autumn friends
 Thou'rt missing and forgot.

The far-famed nightingale, that shares
 Cold public praise from every tongue,
The popular voice of music heirs,
 And injures much thy under-song:
Yet then my walks thy theme salutes;
 I find thee autumn's favoured guest,
Gay piping on the hazel-roots
 Above thy mossy nest.

'Tis wrong that thou shouldst be despised,
 When these gay fickle birds appear;
They sing when summer flowers are prized—
 Thou at the dull and dying year.
Well! let the heedless and the gay
 Bepraise the voice of louder lays,
The joy thou steal'st from Sorrow's day
 Is more to thee than praise.

And could my notes win aught from thine,
 My words but imitate thy lay,
Time could not then his charge resign,
 Nor throw the meanest verse away,
But ever at this mellow time,
 He should thy autumn praise prolong,
As they would share the happy prime
 Of thy eternal song.

THE WOOD ROBIN

By William Thompson Bacon

READER! if thou art sadden'd with the ills
That crowd around thy pathway; if thy heart
Has ever felt the ingratitude of earth,
Which made thee wish to leave it; and if thou
Art one still pure in feeling, and canst find
A bliss in solitude, or aught that's there
Come to these woods. We will sing here together,
A song, a song I learn'd among them once
When but a boy, a time when poetry
Was worshipp'd as we worship some sweet dream.

"Ere yet the golden sun his course renews,
And softest daybreak glimmers in the east,
Clear, deep, and mellow, shrills the robin's note,
And hails the opening day. From some tall bough,
The highest of the elm, or gaudy maple,
He pours his plaint, and to the ear of Morn
Makes gladsome music. From his couch the woodman
Starts at the well-know summons, and goes forth;
As he hies him to his task, more loud
The song comes through the arches of the grove.
And now, while loudly the sonorous axe
Fills with deep voice the solitude, his ear
Detects the hymn, between each loud response,
His friend began before him ; louder still,
And louder yet again, until the sun

73

Bursts through the congregated mass of clouds,
And sends his gladd'ning glory o'er the world.
Meanwhile the woodman pauses at his task,
Shading with brawny hand his swarthy brow;
And, circling all the wood with his keen eye,
He spies at last the little chorister,
Perch'd on the neighb'ring hill-top, or the ash.
Sweet is his note ! Sweet in the early Spring,
When hawthorns bud, and o'er the dewy lea
Daisies spring freshly ! Sweet in summer hours,
When from the apple tree, or prickly pear,
It flows mellifluous ! But sweeter far
Its soothing alternation, when the winds
Weave withered chaplets for old Autumn's brow;
When trees cast down their fruitage, and the woods
Assume the gorgeous livery of decay.
Then doth he leave the tall elm's topmost twig,
And in the hazle hedge, or dog-wood copse,
With faint strain, listless, while away the time.
Plaintive, yet sadly sweet, still is his song,
And sings he, as if half afraid to hear
His own shrill pipe ; and, gentler now become,
(Constrain'd by hunger) where the thresher plies
The noisy flail, he hovers, half at ease,
And half distrustful, with the barn-door tribe.
There from the ridge, he swoops into the croft,
Swift on the scattered grain ; yet quickly thence
Remounts, awed by the strut of chanticleer;
Though soon alights again in desperate chance.
For hunger drives the lion from his lair,
And makes the pard and thirsty tiger tame.

His is the sweetest note in all our woods.
The whistle of the meadow-lark is sweet,
The blackbird's rapid chant fills all the vale,

And touchingly sweet the unincumbered song
That the thrush warbles in the green-wood shade;
Yet is the robin still our sweetest bird,
And beautiful as sweet. His ruddy breast
When poised on high, struck by the unrisen sun,
Glows from its altitude, and to the sight
Presents a burning vestiture of gold;
And his dark pinions, softly spread, improved
By contrast shame, the blackbird's jetty plumes.
Less wild than others of the tuneful choir,
Oft on the tree that shades the farmer's hut,
Close by his door, the little architect
Fixes his home,— though field-groves, and the woods,
Where the small streams murmur sweetly, loves he most.
Who seeks his nest may find it deftly hid
In fork of branching elm, or poplar shade;
And sometimes on the lawn; though rarely he,
The one that sings the sweetest, chooses thus
His habitation. Seek for it in deep
And tangled hollows, up some pretty brook,
That, prattling o'er the loose white pebbles, chides
The echoes with a soft monotony
Of softest music. There, upon the bough
That arches it, of fragrance-breathing birch,
Or kalmia branching in unnumbered forms,
He builds his moss-lined dwelling. First, he lays,
Transverse, dried bents picked from the forest walks;
Or in the glen, where downward with fell force
The mountain torrent rushes,—these all coated
With slime unsightly. Soon the builder shows
An instinct far surpassing human skill,
And lines it with a layer of soft wool,
Picked from the thorn where brushed the straggled flock;
Or with an intertexture of soft hairs,
Or moss, or feathers. Finally, complete,—

The usual list of eggs appear, — and lo!
Four in the whole, and softly tinged with blue.
And now the mother-bird the livelong day
Sits on her charge, nor leaves it for her mate,
Save just to dip her bill into the stream,
Or gather needful sustenance. Meanwhile,
The mate, assiduous, guards that mother-bird
Patient upon her nest; and, at her side,
Or overhead, or on the adverse bank,
Nestled, he all the tedious time beguiles,
Wakes his wild notes, and sings the hours away.

But soon again new duties wake the pair;
Their young appear. Love knocking at their hearts,
Alert they start, as by sure instinct led,—
That beautiful divinity in birds!
And now they hop along the forest edge,
Or dive into the ravines of the woods,
Or roam the fields, or skim the mossy bank
Shading some runnel with its antique forms,
Pecking for sustenance. Or now they mount
Into mid-air; or poise on half-shut wing,
Skimming for insects in the dewy beam,
Gayly disporting; or now, sweeping down
Where the wild brook flows on with ceaseless laughter,
Moisten their bills awhile, then soar away.
And so they weary out the needful hours,
Preaching, meanwhile, sound lesson unto man!
Till plump, and fledged, their little ones essay
Their native element. At first they fail:
Flutter awhile; then, screaming, sink plump down,
Prizes for school-boys. Yet the more escape;
And, wiser grown and stronger, soon their wings
Obedient send they forth; when, confident,
They try the forest tops, or skim the flood,

Or fly up in the skirts of the white clouds, —
Till, all at once, they start, a mirthful throng,
Burst into voice, and the wide forest rings!

TO A ROBIN

By Hannah Flagg Gould

Robin, robin, sing to me,
And I'll gladly suffer thee
Thus to breakfast in the tree,
On the ruddy cherry.
Soon as thou hast swallowed it,
How I love to see thee flit
To another twig, and sit
Singing there so merry!

It was kind in thee to fly
Near my window; and to try
There to raise thy notes so high,
As to break my slumbers.
Robin, half the cheering power
Of this bright and lovely hour,
While I pluck the dewy flower,
Comes from thy sweet numbers.

And thou wast an honest bird,
Thus to let thy voice be heard,
Asking in the plainest word
Thou could'st utter, whether
Those, who owned it, would allow
Thee to take upon the bough
Thy repast, and sit, as now,
Smoothing down thy feathers.

Who, that hears the mellow note
From my robin's little throat
On the air of morning float,
Could desire to still her?
Who her beauty can behold,
And consent to have it told
That he had a heart so cold,
As to try to kill her?

THE ROBIN'S HYMN

By Hannah Flagg Gould

My maker, I know not the place of thy home;
If 't is earth or the sky, or the sea.
I only can tell, that wherever I roam
I've still a kind father in thee.

I feel that, at night, when I go to my rest,
Thy wings all around me are flung.
And peaceful I sleep while the down of thy breast
Is o'er me, as mine, o'er my young.

And when in the morning I open my eye,
I find thou hast long been awake.
Thy beautiful plumage seems spread o'er the sky,
And painted again on the lake.

Thy breath has gone into the buds; and the flowers
Have opened to thee on their stems.
And thou the bright dew-drops hast sent down in showers
To glitter like thousands of gems.

Thy voice with the notes that can only be thine —
A music 't is gladness to hear,
Comes through the green boughs of the oak and the pine,
And falls sweet and soft on my ear.

And many a time hast thou stood between me
And the arrow, that aimed at my heart.
For, though in a form that my eye could not see,
I know thou hast parried the dart.

I drink from the drops on the grass and the vine,
And gratefully gather my food.
I feel thou hast plenty for me and for mine;—
That all things declare thou art good.

My Father, thy pinions are ever unfurled,
With brightness no changes can dim!
My Maker, thy home is all over the world.
Thou'lt hear then, thy Robin's low hymn!

THE ROBIN

By Jones Very

Thou need'st not flutter from thy half-built nest,
Whene'er thou hear'st man's hurrying feet go by,
Fearing his eye for harm may on thee rest,
Or he thy young unfinished cottage spy;
All will not heed thee on that swinging bough,
Nor care that round thy shelter spring the leaves,
Nor watch thee on the pool's wet margin now
For clay to plaster straws thy cunning weaves;
All will not hear thy sweet out-pouring joy,
That with morn's stillness blends the voice of song,
For over-anxious cares their souls employ,
That else upon thy music borne along
And the light wings of heart-ascending prayer
Had learned that Heaven is pleased thy simple joys to share.

TO A REDBREAST

IN SICKNESS

By William Wordsworth

STAY, little cheerful Robin! stay,
  And at my casement sing,
Though it should prove a farewell lay
  And this our parting spring.

Though I, alas! may ne'er enjoy
  The promise in thy song;
A charm, 'that' thought can not destroy,
  Doth to thy strain belong.

Methinks that in my dying hour
  Thy song would still be dear,
And with a more than earthly power
  My passing Spirit cheer.

Then, little Bird, this boon confer,
  Come, and my requiem sing,
Nor fail to be the harbinger
  Of everlasting Spring.

TO ROBIN REDBREAST

By George Meredith

MERRILY 'mid the faded leaves,
   O Robin of the bright red breast!
Cheerily over the Autumn eaves,
   Thy note is heard, bonny bird;
Sent to cheer us, and kindly endear us
     To what would be a sorrowful time
     Without thee in the weltering clime:
     Merry art thou in the boughs of the lime,
       While thy fadeless waistcoat glows on thy breast,
       In Autumn's reddest livery drest.

A merry song, a cheery song!
     In the boughs above, on the sward below,
Chirping and singing the live day long,
     While the maple in grief sheds its fiery leaf,
And all the trees waning, with bitter complaining,
     Chestnut, and elm, and sycamore,
     Catch the wild gust in their arms, and roar
     Like the sea on a stormy shore,
       Till wailfully they let it go,
       And weep themselves naked and weary with woe.

Merrily, cheerily, joyously still
　　Pours out the crimson-crested tide.
The set of the season burns bright on the hill,
　　Where the foliage dead falls yellow and red,
Picturing vainly, but foretelling plainly
　　The wealth of cottage warmth that comes
　　When the frost gleams and the blood numbs,
　　And then, bonny Robin, I'll spread thee out crumbs
　　　In my garden porch for thy redbreast pride,
　　　The song and the ensign of dear fireside.

ROBIN REDBREAST

By William Allingham

Goodbye, goodbye to summer!
  For summer's nearly done;
The garden smiling faintly,
  Cool breezes in the sun;

Our thrushes now are silent,
  Our swallows flown away —
But Robin's here, in coat of brown,
  With ruddy breast-knot gay.

Robin, Robin Redbreast,
  O Robin dear!
Robin singing sweetly
  In the falling of the year.

Bright yellow, red, and orange,
  The leaves come down in hosts;
The trees are Indian princes,
  But soon they'll turn to ghosts;

The leathery pears and apples
  Hang russet on the bough,
It's autumn, autumn, autumn late,
  'Twill soon be winter now.

Robin, Robin Redbreast,
　O Robin dear!
And what will this poor Robin do?
　For pinching days are near.

The fireside for the cricket,
　The wheatstack for the mouse,
When trembling night-winds whistle
　And moan all round the house;

The frosty ways like iron,
　The branches plumed with snow —
Alas! in winter, dead and dark,
　Where can poor Robin go?

Robin, Robin Redbreast,
　O Robin dear!
And a crumb of bread for Robin,
　His little heart to cheer.

HOW THE ROBIN CAME

AN ALGONQUIN LEGEND

By John Greenleaf Whittier

Happy young friends, sit by me,
Under May's blown apple-tree,
While these home-birds in and out
Through the blossoms flit about.
Hear a story, strange and old,
By the wild red Indians told,
How the robin came to be:

Once a great chief left his son,—
Well-beloved, his only one,—
When the boy was well-nigh grown,
In the trial-lodge alone.
Left for tortures long and slow
Youths like him must undergo,
Who their pride of manhood test,
Lacking water, food, and rest.
Seven days the fast he kept,
Seven nights he never slept.
Then the young boy, wrung with pain,
Weak from nature's overstrain,
Faltering, moaned a low complaint
"Spare me, father, for I faint!"
But the chieftain, haughty-eyed,

Hid his pity in his pride.
"You shall be a hunter good,
Knowing never lack of food;
You shall be a warrior great,
Wise as fox and strong as bear;
Many scalps your belt shall wear,
If with patient heart you wait
Bravely till your task is done.
Better you should starving die
Than that boy and squaw should cry
Shame upon your father's son!"

When next morn the sun's first rays
Glistened on the hemlock sprays,
Straight that lodge the old chief sought,
And boiled sainp and moose meat brought.
"Rise and eat, my son!" he said.
Lo, he found the poor boy dead!

As with grief his grave they made,
And his bow beside him laid,
Pipe, and knife, and wampum-braid,
On the lodge-top overhead,
Preening smooth its breast of red
And the brown coat that it wore,
Sat a bird, unknown before.
And as if with human tongue,
"Mourn me not," it said, or sung;
"I, a bird, am still your son,
Happier than if hunter fleet,
Or a brave, before your feet
Laying scalps in battle won.
Friend of man, my song shall cheer
Lodge and corn-land; hovering near,
To each wigwam I shall bring

Tidings of the corning spring;
Every child my voice shall know
In the moon of melting snow,
When the maple's red bud swells,
And the wind-flower lifts its bells.
As their fond companion
Men shall henceforth own your son,
And my song shall testify
That of human kin am I."

Thus the Indian legend saith
How, at first, the robin came
With a sweeter life from death,
Bird for boy, and still the same.
If my young friends doubt that this
Is the robin's genesis,
Not in vain is still the myth
If a truth be found therewith
Unto gentleness belong
Gifts unknown to pride and wrong;
Happier far than hate is praise,—
He who sings than he who slays.

ROBIN
REDBREAST'S REWARD

By James Ryder Randall

THE Saviour, bowed beneath his cross, climbed up the dreary hill,
And from the agonizing wreath ran many a crimson rill;
The cruel Roman thrust him on with unrelenting hand,
Till, staggering slowly mid the crowd, He fell upon the sand.

A little bird that warbled near, that memorable day,
Flitted around and strove to wrench one single thorn away;
The cruel spike impaled his breast, — and thus, 't is sweetly said,
The Robin has his silver vest incarnadined with red.
Ah, Jesu! Jesu! Son of man! My dolor and my sighs
Reveal the lesson taught by this winged Ishmael of the skies.
I, in the palace of delight or cavern of despair,
Have plucked no thorns from thy dear brow, but planted
  thousands there!

THE ENGLISH ROBIN

By Harrison Weir

SEE yon robin on the spray;
　Look ye how his tiny form
Swells, as when his merry lay
　Gushes forth amid the storm.

Though the snow is falling fast,
　Speckling o'er his coat with white, —
Though loud roars the chilly blast,
　And the evening's lost in night, —

Yet from out the darkness dreary
　Cometh still that cheerful note;
Praiseful aye, and never weary,
　Is that little warbling throat.

Thank him for his lesson's sake,
　Thank God's gentle minstrel there,
Who, when storms make others quake,
　Sings of days that brighter were.

THE ROBIN

By John Greenleaf Whittier

MY old Welsh neighbor over the way
  Crept slowly out in the sun of spring,
Pushed from her ears the locks of gray,
  And listened to hear the robins sing.

Her grandson, playing at marbles, stopped,
  And, cruel in sport as boys will be,
Tossed a stone at the bird, who hopped
  From bough to bough in the apple-tree.

"Nay!" said the grandmother; "have you not heard,
  My poor, bad boy! of the fiery pit,
And how, drop by drop, this merciful bird
  Carries the water that quenches it?

"He brings cool dew in his little bill,
  And lets it fall on the souls of sin:
You can see the mark on his red breast still
  Of fires that scorch as he drops it in.

"My poor Bron rhuddyn! my breast-burned bird,
  Singing so sweetly from limb to limb,
Very dear to the heart of Our Lord
  Is he who pities the lost like Him!"

"Amen!" I said to the beautiful myth;
  "Sing, bird of God, in my heart as well:
Each good thought is a drop wherewith
  To cool and lessen the fires of hell.

"Prayers of love like rain-drops fall,
  Tears of pity are cooling dew,
And dear to the heart of Our Lord are all
  Who suffer like Him in the good they do!"

THE ROBIN'S NEST

By Phoebe Cary

JENNY BROWN has as pretty a house of her own
   As ever a bird need to want, I should think;
And the sheltering vine that about it had grown,
   Half hid it in green leaves and roses of pink.

As she never looked shabby, or seemed out of date,
   It was surely enough, though she had but one dress;
And Robin, the fellow she took for her mate,
   Was quite constant — that is, for a Robin, I guess.

Jenny Brown had four birdies, the cunningest things
   That ever peeped back to a motherbird's call;
That only could flutter their soft downy wings,
   And open their mouths to take food — that was all.

Now I dare say you think she was happy and gay,
   And she was almost always contented; but yet,
Though I know you will hardly believe what I say,
   Sometimes she would ruffle her feathers and fret.

One day, tired of flying about in the heat,
   She came home in her crossest and sulkiest mood;
And though she brought back not a morsel to eat,
   She pecked little Robin for crying for food.

Just then Robin came and looked in through the trees,
  And saw with a quick glance that all was not right,
But he sung out as cheerful and gay as you please:
  "Why, Jenny, dear Jenny, how are you to-night?"

It made her more angry to see him so calm,
  While she suffered all that a bird could endure;
And she answered, "'How am I?' who cares how I am?
  It isn't you, Robin, for one, I am sure!

"You know I've been tied here day in and day out,
  Till I'm tired almost of my home and my life,
While you — you go carelessly roving about,
  And singing to every one else but your wife."

Then Robin replied: "Little reason you've got
  To complain of me, Jenny; wherever I roam
I still think of you, and your quieter lot,
  And wish 't was my place to stay here at home.

"And as to my singing, I give you my word,
  'T is in concert, and always in public, beside;
For excepting yourself, there is no ladybird
  Knows the softest and lovingest notes I have tried.

"And, Jenny," — and here he spoke tenderly quite,
  As with head drooped aside he drew nearer and stood, —
"I heard some sad news as I came home to-night,
  About our poor neighbors that live in the wood.

"You know Nelly Jay, that wild, thoughtless young thing,
  Who takes in her children and home no delight,
But early and late is abroad on the wing,
  To chatter and gossip from morning till night, —

"Well, yesterday, just after noon, she went out,
   And strayed till the sun had gone down in the west;
Complaining to some of her friends, I've no doubt,
   Of the trouble she had taking care of her nest;

"And her sweet little Nelly, — you've seen her, my dear,
   The brightest and sprightliest bird of them all,
The age of our Jenny, I think, very near,
   Tumbled out of the nest and was killed by the fall.

"I saw the poor thing lying stiff on the ground,
   With its little wing broke and the film o'er its eyes,
While the mother was flying distractedly round
   And startling the wood with her piteous cries.

"As I stopped, just to say a kind, comforting word,
   I thought how my own home was guarded and blessed;
For, Jenny, my darling, my beauty, my bird,
   I knew I should find you content in the nest!

"And how are our birdies? — the dear little things;
   How softly and snugly asleep they are laid;
But don't fold them quite so close under your wings,
   Or you'll kill them with kindness, my pet, I'm afraid.

"And, Jenny, I'll stay with them now, — nay, I must,
   While you go out a moment, and take the fresh air;
You sit here too much by yourself, I mistrust,
   And are quite overburdened with work and with care.

"What, you don't want to go! you want nothing so long
   As your dear little ones and your Robin are here?
Then I'll stay with you, Jenny, and sing the old song
   I sang when I courted you — shall I, my dear?"

THE GOLDEN-ROBIN'S NEST

By John White Chadwick

THE golden-robin came to build his nest
High in the elm-tree's ever-nodding crest;
All the long day, upon his task intent,
Backward and forward busily he went,

Gathering from far and near the tiny shreds
That birdies weave for little birdies' beds;
Now bits of grass, now bits of vagrant string,
And now some queerer, dearer sort of thing.

For on the lawn, where he was wont to come
In search of stuff to build his pretty home,
We dropped one day a lock of golden hair
Which our wee darling easily could spare;

And close beside it tenderly we placed
A lock that had the stooping shoulders graced
Of her old grandsire; it was white as snow,
Or cherry-trees when they are all ablow.

Then throve the golden-robin's work apace;
Hundreds of times he sought the lucky place
Where sure, he thought, in his bird-fashion dim,
Wondrous provision had been made for him.

103

Both locks, the white and golden, disappeared;
The nest was finished, and the brood was reared;
And then there came a pleasant summer's day
When the last golden-robin flew away.

Ere long, in triumph, from its leafy height,
We bore the nest so wonderfully dight,
And saw how prettily the white and gold
Made warp and woof of many a gleaming fold.

But when again the golden-robins came,
Cleaving the orchards with their breasts aflame,
Grandsire's white locks and baby's golden head
Were lying low, both in one grassy bed.

And so more dear than ever is the nest
Taken from the elm-tree's ever nodding crest.
Little the golden-robin thought how rare
A thing he wrought of white and golden hair!

A NEW VERSION
OF WHY THE RED
ROBIN'S BREAST IS RED

By Paul Hamilton Hayne

KNOW you why the robin's breast
Gleameth of a dusky red,
Like the lustre mid the stars
Of the potent planet Mars?
'Tis — a monkish myth has said —
Owing to his cordial heart;
For, long since, he took the part
Of those hapless children, sent
Hadean-ward for punishment;
And, to quench the fierce desire,
Bred in them by ruthless fire,
Brought on tiny bill and wing,
Water from some earthly spring,
Which in misty droplets fell
O'er their dwelling of unrest,
While the sufferer's faces grew
Softer 'neath the healing dew!

But, too far within that hell
Venturing, some malicious fiend,
A small devil hardly weaned,
Seized bold Robin in his claw,
Striving thro' the flames to draw
His poor body, until fled
Sight of eyes and sense of head,
Scorched he lay and almost dead!

Then, a child whose tongue and brow,
Robin's help had cooled but now,
Clutched the baby-fiend in ire,
And in gulfs of his own fire
Soused the vile misshapen elf.

Fluttering upwards, scarce himself,
After all the pain and fear
Of his horrid sojourn there
In that realm of flame and smoke,
Lo! earth's happy sunlight broke
On the bird's dazed view at last;
But the ordeal he had passed
Left a flame-spot widely spread
Where the wind-blown feathers part
Just above his loyal heart.
So the robin's breast is red!

BLEAK WEATHER

By Ella Wheeler Wilcox

Dear Love, where the red lilies blossomed and grew
   The white snows are falling;
And all through the woods where I wandered with you
   The loud winds are calling;
And the robin that piped to us tune upon tune,
   Neath the oak, you remember,
O'er hilltop and forest has followed the June
   And left us December.

He has left like a friend who is true in the sun
   And false in the shadows;
He has found new delights in the land where he 's gone.
   Greener woodlands and meadows.
Let him go! what care we? let the snow shroud the lea,
   Let it drift on the heather;
We can sing through it all: I have you, you have me,
   And we'll laugh at the weather.

The old year may die and a new year be born
   That is bleaker and colder:
It cannot dismay us; we dare it, we scorn,
   For our love makes us bolder.
Ah, Robin! sing loud on your far-distant lea,
   You friend in fair weather!
But here is a song sung that fuller of glee
   By two warm hearts together.

TAMPA ROBINS

By Sidney Lanier

THE robin laughed in the orange-tree:
"Ho, windy North, a fig for thee:
While breasts are red and wings are bold
And green trees wave us globes of gold,
   Time's scythe shall reap but bliss for me
   — Sunlight, song, and the orange-tree.

Burn, golden globes in leafy sky,
My orange-planets: crimson I
Will shine and shoot among the spheres
(Blithe meteor that no mortal fears)
   And thrid the heavenly orange-tree
   With orbits bright of minstrelsy.

If that I hate wild winter's spite —
The gibbet trees, the world in white,
The sky but gray wind over a grave —
Why should I ache, the season's slave?
   I'll sing from the top of the orange-tree
   Gramercy, winter's tyranny.

I'll south with the sun, and keep my clime;
My wing is king of the summer-time;
My breast to the sun his torch shall hold;
And I'll call down through the green and gold
   Time, take thy scythe, reap bliss for me,
   Bestir thee under the orange-tree."

TAMPA, FLORIDA, 1877.

THE ROBIN REDBREAST

By Mathilde Blind

THE year's grown songless! No glad pipings thrill
  The hedge-row elms, whose wind-worn branches shower
  Their leaves on the sere grass, where some late flower
In golden chalice hoards the sunlight still.
Our summer guests, whose raptures used to fill
  Each apple-blossomed garth and honeyed bower,
  Have in adversity's inclement hour
Abandoned us to bleak November's chill.

But hearken! Yonder russet bird among
  The crimson clusters of the homely thorn
Still bubbles o'er with little rills of song —
A blending of sweet hope and resignation:
  Even so, when life of love and youth is shorn,
One friend becomes its last, best consolation.

ROBIN'S SECRET

By Katharine Lee Bates

'T IS the blithest, bonniest weather for a bird to flirt a feather,
    For a bird to trill and warble, all his wee red breast a-swell.
I've a secret. You may listen till your blue eyes dance and glisten,
    Little maiden, but I'll never, never, never, never tell.

You'll find no more wary piper, till the strawberries wax riper
    In December than in June — aha! all up and down the dell,
Where my nest is set, for certain, with a pink and snowy curtain,
    East or west, but which I'll never, never, never, never tell.

You may prick me with a thistle, if you ever hear me whistle
    How my brooding mate, whose weariness my carols sweet dispel,
All between the clouds and clover, apple blossoms drooping over,
    Twitters low that I must never, never, never, never tell.

Oh, I swear no closer fellow stains his bill in cherries mellow.
    Tra la la! and tirra lirra! I'm the jauntiest sentinel,
Perched beside my jewel-casket, where lie hidden — don't you ask it,
    For of those three eggs I'll never, never, never, never tell.

Chirp! chirp! chirp! alack! for pity! Who hath marred my
  merry ditty?
    Who hath stirred the scented petals, peeping in where robins dwell?
Oh, my mate! May Heaven defend her! Little maidens' hearts
  are tender,
    And I never, never, never, never, never meant to tell.

113

IF I CAN STOP
ONE HEART FROM BREAKING

By Emily Dickinson

If I can stop one heart from breaking,
I shall not live in vain;
If I can ease one life the aching,
Or cool one pain,
Or help one fainting robin
Unto his nest again,
I shall not live in vain.

MAY-FLOWER

By Emily Dickinson

Pink, small, and punctual,
Aromatic, low,
Covert in April,
Candid in May,

Dear to the moss,
Known by the knoll,
Next to the robin
In every human soul.

Bold little beauty,
Bedecked with thee,
Nature forswears
Antiquity.

IF I SHOULDN'T BE ALIVE

By Emily Dickinson

If I shouldn't be alive
When the robins come,
Give the one in red cravat
A memorial crumb.

If I couldn't thank you,
Being just asleep,
You will know I'm trying
With my granite lip!

THE ROBINS' OTHER NAME

By James Whitcomb Riley

IN the Orchard-Days, when you
Children look like blossoms, too;
Bessie, with her jaunty ways
And trim poise of head and face,
Must have looked superior
Even to the blossoms, — for
Little Winnie once averred
Bessie looked just like the bird
Tilted on the topmost spray
Of the apple boughs in May,
With the redbreast, and the strong,
Clear, sweet warble of his song. —
"I don't know their *name*," Win said —
"I ist *maked* a name instead." —
So forever afterwards
We called robins "Bessie-birds."

A WINTRY SONNET

By Christina Rossetti

A Robin said: The Spring will never come,
  And I shall never care to build again.
A Rosebush said: These frosts are wearisome,
  My sap will never stir for sun or rain.
The half Moon said: These nights are fogged and slow,
  I neither care to wax nor care to wane.
The Ocean said: I thirst from long ago,
  Because earth's rivers cannot fill the main.—
When Springtime came, red Robin built a nest,
  And trilled a lover's song in sheer delight.
  Grey hoarfrost vanished, and the Rose with might
  Clothed her in leaves and buds of crimson core.
The dim Moon brightened. Ocean sunned his crest,
  Dimpled his blue, yet thirsted evermore.

THE ROBIN

By Emily Dickinson

The robin is the one
That interrupts the morn
With hurried, few, express reports
When March is scarcely on.

The robin is the one
That overflows the noon
With her cherubic quantity,
An April but begun.

The robin is the one
That speechless from her nest
Submits that home and certainty
And sanctity are best.

ROBIN'S MISTAKE

By Ella Wheeler Wilcox

WHAT do you think Red Robin
  Found by a mow of hay?
Why, a flask brimful of liquor,
  That the mowers brought that day
To slake their thirst in the hayfield.
  And Robin he shook his head:
"Now I wonder what they call it,
  And how it tastes?" he said.

'I have seen the mowers drink it—
  Why isn't it good for me?
So I'll just draw out the stopper
  And get at the stuff, and see!"
But alas! for the curious Robin,
  One draught, and he burned his throat
From his bill to his poor crop's lining,
  And he could not utter a note.

And his head grew light and dizzy,
  And he staggered left and right,
Tipped over the flask of brandy,
  And spilled it, every mite.
But after awhile he sobered,
  And quietly flew away,
And he never has tasted liquor,
  Or touched it, since that day.

But I heard him say to his kindred,
  In the course of a friendly chat,
"These men think they are above us,
  Yet they drink such stuff as that!
Oh, the poor degraded creatures!
  I am glad I am only a bird!"
Then he flew up over the meadow,
  And that was all I heard.

THE ROBIN IN JANUARY

By Henry Charles Beeching

'Hey robin, jolly robin'

Green again, O green to-day
  Garden lawn, and mossy park;
They have laid a while away
  Winter's ermine cloak; and hark.
Hark, our robin, who but he?
  Singing blithe as blithe can be.

"Tis not passion's melting note,
  Though his breast be red like fire;
Nor can his, like thrush's throat,
  Raise to rapture each desire:
'Tis a song of simplest joy,
  Like the laughter of a boy.

Robin, keep thy happy heart,
  Through the year so well begun:
Live and love, unheard, apart.
  So may we, when Summer's done,
Tired with art and passion-spent,
  Hear and share thy sweet content.

THE ROBIN'S FAREWELL

By Clara Doty Bates

GOOD-BYE, old tree, good-bye!
  I leave my nest with you;
You'll need it when your green leaves die,
  And your apples are fallen too;
Something upon your boughs
  For children to come and see,
If only a bird's deserted house
  Good-bye, old apple tree!

We were friends from the very first,
  When in the chill March air,
Before a single bud had burst,
  I found you bleak and bare.
Even then your branches stirred
  In a kindly, welcoming way,
As if they knew a lonely bird
  Needed some place to stay.

And after that you spread
  The greenest, leafiest roof
That ever sheltered a robin's head,
  Waving, but weather-proof.
And I remember well
  How every gala breeze,
Before your pink-white blossoms fell,
  Brought scores of honey-bees.

They hummed their drowsy tune;
  My mate sang loud and sweet;
And the sun winked, and the quiet moon
  Walked by with silver feet;
While with my mother-wings
  I brooded the eggs of blue,
Till those four red-breast little things
  Grew restless and broke through.

You rocked them every one;
  But now, in the usual way,
They have learned to fly, and would be gone,
  And so, we are off to-day.
More than they dream of now
  They'll miss your lullaby,
Miss every leaf, and twig and bough
  Good-bye, old tree, good-bye!

ROBIN

By John Banister Tabb

COME to me, Robin! The daylight is dying!
  Come to me now!
Come, ere the cypress-tree over me sighing,
Dank with the shadow-tide, circle my brow;
Come, ere oblivion speed to me, flying
  Swifter than thou!

Come to me, Robin! The far echoes waken
  Cold to my cry!
Oh! with the swallow-wing, love overtaken,
Hence to the Echo-land, homeward, to fly!
Thou art my life, Robin. Oh! love-forsaken,
  How can I die?

TO A WOOD-ROBIN

By John Banister Tabb

LO, where the blooming woodland wakes
　From wintry slumbers long,
Thy heart, a bud of silence, breaks
　To ecstasy of song.

HOW DARE
THE ROBINS SING

By Emily Dickinson

How dare the robins sing,
　When men and women hear
Who since they went to their account
　Have settled with the year! —
Paid all that life had earned
　In one consummate bill,
And now, what life or death can do
　Is immaterial.
Insulting is the sun
　To him whose mortal light,
Beguiled of immortality,
　Bequeaths him to the night.
In deference to him
　Extinct be every hum,
Whose garden wrestles with the dew,
　At daybreak overcome!

COMPARISON

By Paul Laurence Dunbar

THE sky of brightest gray seems dark
 To one whose sky was ever white.
To one who never knew a spark,
 Thro' all his life, of love or light,
 The grayest cloud seems overbright.

The robin sounds a beggar's note
 Where one the nightingale has heard,
But he for whom no silver throat
 Its liquid music ever stirred,
 Deems robin still the sweetest bird.

TO THE WOOD-ROBIN (2)

By John Banister Tabb

The wooing air is jubilant with song,
    And blossoms swell
As leaps thy liquid melody along
    The dusky dell,
Where silence, late supreme, foregoes her wonted spell.

Ah, whence, in sylvan solitudes remote,
    Hast learned the lore
That breeds delight in every echoing note,
    The woodlands o'er;
As when through slanting sun descends the quickening shower?

Thy hermitage is peopled with the dreams
    That gladden sleep;
Here fancy dallies with delirious themes
    'Mid shadows deep,
Till eyes, unused to tears, with wild emotion weep.

We rise, alas, to find out visions fled!
    But thine remain.
Night weaves of golden harmonies the thread,
    And fills thy brain
With joys that overflow in love's awakening strain.

Yet thou, from mortal influence apart,
    Seek'st naught of praise;
The empty plaudits of the emptier heart
    Taint not thy lays:
Thy Maker's smile alone thy tuneful bosom sways.

Teach me, thou warbling eremite, to sing
    Thy rhapsody;
Nor borne on vain ambition's vaunting wing,
    But led of thee
To rise from earthly dreams to hymn eternity.

OWL AGAINST ROBIN

By Sidney Lanier

FROWNING, the owl in the oak complained him
Sore, that the song of the robin restrained him
Wrongly of slumber, rudely of rest.
"From the north, from the east, from the south and the west,
Woodland, wheat-field, corn-field, clover,
Over and over and over and over,
Five o'clock, ten o'clock, twelve, or seven,
Nothing but robin-songs heard under heaven:
       How can we sleep?

Peep! you whistle, and *cheep! cheep! cheep!*
Oh, peep, if you will, and buy, if 'tis cheap,
And have done; for an owl must sleep.
Are ye singing for fame, and who shall be first?
Each day's the same, yet the last is worst,
And the summer is cursed with the silly outburst
Of idiot red-breasts peeping and cheeping
By day, when all honest birds ought to be sleeping.
Lord, what a din! And so out of all reason.
Have ye not heard that each thing hath its season?
Night is to work in, night is for play-time;
       Good heavens, not day-time!

A vulgar flaunt is the flaring day,
The impudent, hot, unsparing day,
That leaves not a stain nor a secret untold, —
Day the reporter, — the gossip of old, —
Deformity's tease, — man's common scold —
Poh! Shut the eyes, let the sense go numb
When day down the eastern way has come.
'Tis clear as the moon (by the argument drawn
From Design) that the world should retire at dawn.
Day kills. The leaf and the laborer breathe
Death in the sun, the cities seethe,
The mortal black marshes bubble with heat
And puff up pestilence; nothing is sweet
Has to do with the sun: even virtue will taint
(Philosophers say) and manhood grow faint
In the lands where the villainous sun has sway
Through the livelong drag of the dreadful day.
What Eden but noon-light stares it tame,
Shadowless, brazen, forsaken of shame?
For the sun tells lies on the landscape, — now
Reports me the *what*, unrelieved with the how, —
As messengers lie, with the facts alone,
Delivering the word and withholding the tone.

But oh, the sweetness, and oh, the light
Of the high-fastidious night!
Oh, to awake with the wise old stars —
The cultured, the careful, the Chesterfield stars,
That wink at the work-a-day fact of crime
And shine so rich through the ruins of time
That Baalbec is finer than London; oh,
To sit on the bough that zigzags low
        By the woodland pool,
And loudly laugh at man, the fool
That vows to the vulgar sun; oh, rare,

To wheel from the wood to the window where
A day-worn sleeper is dreaming of care,
And perch on the sill and straightly stare
Through his visions; rare, to sail
Aslant with the hill and a-curve with the vale, —

To flit down the shadow-shot-with-gleam,
Betwixt hanging leaves and starlit stream,
Hither, thither, to and fro,
Silent, aimless, dayless, slow
(*Aimless? Field-mice?* True, they're slain,
But the night-philosophy hoots at pain,
Grips, eats quick, and drops the bones
In the water beneath the bough, nor moans
At the death life feeds on.) Robin, pray
  Come away, come away
To the cultus of night. Abandon the day.
Have more to think and have less to say.
And *cannot* you walk now? Bah! don't hop!
  Stop!
Look at the owl, scarce seen, scarce heard,
O irritant, iterant, maddening bird!"

BALTIMORE, 1880.

TO THE FIRST ROBIN

By Ray Clarke Rose

O robin, sing your first spring song to me!
  Since autumn trailed her scarlet robes in dust,
  And in her hapless passion, burned with rust
The ripened fields, I 've looked in every tree,
In every bush that plumes above the lea,
  For you, dear friend with umber-tinted bust!
  And through the frigid months, with cheerful trust
I've waited for your vernal jubilee,
Till now, at last, where yet the snowy foam
  Of winter tempests flecks the chastened lawn,
    I see you standing, triumph-voiced and strong,
With keen bill prodding in the grassy loam!—
  Sweet songster with the breast like russet dawn,
    Mount yonder tree and carol me a song!

ROBIN REDBREAST

By John Banister Tabb

When Christ was taken from the rood,
  One thorn upon the ground,
Still moistened with the Precious Blood,
  An early robin found,
And wove it crosswise in his nest,
Where, lo, it reddened all his breast!

ON A REDBREAST
SINGING AT THE GRAVE OF PLATO
(IN THE GROVE OF ACADEME)

By William Sharp

The rose of gloaming everywhere!
And through the silence cool and sweet
A song falls through the golden air
And stays my feet—
For there! . . .
This very moment surely I have heard
The sudden, swift, incalculable word
That takes me o'er the foam
Of these empurpling, dim Ionian seas,
That takes me home
To where
Far on an isle of the far Hebrides
Sits on a spray of gorse a little home-sweet bird.

The great white Attic poplars rise,
And down their tremulous stairs I hear
Light airs and delicate sighs.
Even here
Outside this grove of ancient olive-trees,
Close by this trickling murmuring stream,
Was laid long, long ago, men say,
That lordly Prince of Peace
Who loved to wander here from day to day,
Plato, who from this Academe

Sent radiant dreams sublime
Across the troubled seas of time,
Dreams that not yet are passed away,
Nor faded grown, nor grey,
But white, immortal are
As that great star
That yonder hangs above Hymettos' brow.

But now
It is not he, the Dreamer of the Dream,
That holds my thought.
Greece, Plato, and the Academe
Are all forgot:
It is as though I am unloosed by hands:
My heart aches for the grey-green seas
That hold a lonely isle
Far in the Hebrides,
An isle where all day long
The redbreast's song
Goes fluting on the wind o'er lonely sands.

So beautiful, so beautiful
Is Hellas, here.
Divinely clear
The mellow golden air,
Filled, as a rose is full,
Of delicate flame:
And oh the secret tides of thought and dream
That haunt this slow Kephisian stream!
But yet more sweet, more beautiful, more dear
The secret tides of memory and thought
That link me to the far-off shore
For which I long—
Greece, Plato, and the Academe forgot
For a robin's song!

TO THE
OREGON ROBIN

By John Burroughs

O varied thrush! O robin strange!
  Behold my mute surprise.
Thy form and flight I long have known,
  But not this new disguise.

I do not know thy slaty coat,
  Thy vest with darker zone;
I'm puzzled by thy recluse ways
  And song in monotone.

I left thee 'mid my orchard's bloom,
  When May had crowned the year;
Thy nest was on the apple-bough,
  Where rose thy carol clear.

Thou lurest now through fragrant shades,
  Where hoary spruces grow;
Where floor of moss infolds the foot,
  Like depths of fallen snow.

I follow fast, or pause alert,
  To spy out thy retreat;
Or see thee perched on tree or shrub,
  Where field and forest meet.

Thy voice is like a hermit's reed
  That solitude beguiles;
Again 'tis is like a silver bell
  Atune in forest aisles.

Throw off, throw off this masquerade
  And don thy ruddy vest,
And let me find thee, as of old,
  Beside thy orchard nest.

WHY ROBIN'S BREAST IS RED

By James R. Randall

The Saviour bowed beneath his cross,
  Clomb up the dreary hill,
While from his agonizing brow
  Ran many a crimson rill.
The brawny Roman thrust him on
  With unrelenting hand,
Till, staggering slowly 'mid the crowd,
  He sank upon the sand.

A little song-bird hovering near,
  That immemorial day,
Fluttered around and strove to wrench
  One single thorn away.
The cruel spike impaled his breast,
  And thus, 'tis sweetly said,
The robin has his silver vest
  Incarnadined with red!

Ah, Jesu! Jesu! Prince of Peace,
  My dolor and my sighs
Reveal the lesson taught by this
  Winged Ishmael of the skies.
I, in the palace of delight,
  Or caverns of despair,
Have plucked no thorns from thy dear brow,
  But planted thousands there!

FLOWER AND THORN

By Thomas Bailey Aldrich

Four bluish eggs all in the moss!
  Soft-lined home on the cherry-bough!
Life is trouble, and love is loss—
  There's only one robin now.

O robin up in the cherry-tree,
  Singing your soul away,
Great is the grief befallen me,
  And how can you be so gay?

Long ago when you cried in the nest,
  The last of the sickly brood,
Scarcely a pinfeather warming your breast,
  Who was it brought you food?

Who said, "Music, come fill his throat,
  Or ever the May be fled"?
Who was it loved the low sweet note
  And the bosom's sea-shell red?

Who said, "Cherries, grow ripe and big,
  Black and ripe for this bird of mine"?
How little bright-bosom bends the twig,
  Sipping the black-heart's wine!

Now that my days and nights are woe,
  Now that I weep for love's dear sake—
There you go singing away as though
  Never a heart could break!

THE ROBIN

By Dora Sigerson Shorter

ALL day and every day,
Upon a hawthorn spray,
   Early and late,
A redbreast robin sings,
And flirts his nut-brown wings,
   Beside my gate.

A hawk hangs in the sky,
A weasel low doth spy
   From out the grass,
This bird that had no care
Pipes sweet his happy prayer
   To all who pass.

All night and every night,
He, hidden from our sight,
   Awaits the morn;
The seeking owl swoops low,
The evil rat doth go
   Beneath the thorn.

But redbreast robin sings,
Flirting his nut-brown wings,
    When dawn is here.
Upon a hawthorn spray
He sings of holiday,
    And hath no fear.

All day and every day
I seek his prayer to say
    And understand,
Because the hawk that flies,
The stoat who hides and spies,
    Leave me unmanned.

And in the dark of night
The owl in silent flight
    Will swoop and dart,
The evil rat doth creep
When comes reluctant sleep,
    To tear my heart.

But redbreast robin sings,
And shakes his dew-wet wings,
    Nor sighs, 'Alas.'
This bird that had no care
Pipes forth his happy prayer
    To all who pass.

ROBIN'S MATE

By Ella Gilbert Ives

Everybody praises Robin,
  Singing early, singing late;
But who ever thinks of saying
  A good word for Robin's Mate?

Yet she's everything to Robin,
  Silent partner though she be;
Source and theme and inspiration
  Of each madrigal and glee.

For as she with mute devotion
  Shapes and curves the plastic nest,
Fashioning a tiny cradle,
  With the pressure of her breast;

So the love in that soft bosom
  Moulds his being as 'twere clay,
Prints upon his breast the music
  Of his most impassioned lay.

And, when next you praise the Robin
  Flinging wide the tuneful gate
To his eager brood of love-notes
  Don't forget the Robin's Mate.

ROBIN REDBREAST

By William Henry Davies

Robin on a leafless bough,
　Lord in Heaven, how he sings!
Now cold Winter's cruel Wind
　Makes playmates of poor, dead things.

How he sings for joy this morn!
　How his breast doth pant and glow!
Look you how he stands and sings,
　Half-way up his legs in snow!

If these crumbs of bread were pearls,
　And I had no bread at home,
He should have them for that song;
　Pretty Robin Redbreast, Come.

THE ROBIN

By Thomas Hardy

WHEN up aloft
I fly and fly,
I see in pools
The shining sky,
And a happy bird
Am I, am I!

When I descend
Towards their brink
I stand, and look,
And stoop, and drink,
And bathe my wings,
And chink and prink.

When winter frost
Makes earth as steel
I search and search
But find no meal,
And most unhappy
Then I feel.

But when it lasts,
And snows still fall,
I get to feel
No grief at all,
For I turn to a cold stiff
Feathery ball!

HOME

By Francis Ledwidge

A BURST of sudden wings at dawn,
Faint voices in a dreamy noon,
Evenings of mist and murmurings,
And nights with rainbows of the moon.

And through these things a wood-way dim,
And waters dim, and slow sheep seen
On uphill paths that wind away
Through summer sounds and harvest green.

This is a song a robin sang
This morning on a broken tree,
It was about the little fields
That call across the world to me.

A SPRINGTIME WISH

By Isabel Ecclestone Mackay

O, TO be a robin
  In the Spring!
When the fleeting days of April
  Are a-wing,
And the air is sweet with knowing
Where the hidden buds are growing,
And the merry winds are going
  Wandering!

O, to be a robin
  With a nest
Built upon the budding branches—
  East or West!
Just to swing and sway and dangle,
Far from earth and all its tangle,
Joining in the gay bird-jangle,
  With a zest!

O, to be a robin
  Just to sing!
Not to have the pain of hating
  Anything—
Just to race the foremost swallow
Over hill and over hollow—
And the joy of life to follow
  Through the Spring.

ROBIN'S MISTAKE

By Ella Wheeler Wilcox

WHAT do you think Red Robin
　　Found by a mow of hay?
Why, a flask brimful of liquor,
　　That the mowers brought that day
To slake their thirst in the hayfield.
　　And Robin he shook his head:
"Now I wonder what they call it,
　　And how it tastes?" he said.

'I have seen the mowers drink it—
　　Why isn't it good for me?
So I'll just draw out the stopper
　　And get at the stuff, and see!"
But alas! for the curious Robin,
　　One draught, and he burned his throat
From his bill to his poor crop's lining,
　　And he could not utter a note.

And his head grew light and dizzy,
　　And he staggered left and right,
Tipped over the flask of brandy,
　　And spilled it, every mite.
But after awhile he sobered,
　　And quietly flew away,
And he never has tasted liquor,
　　Or touched it, since that day.

But I heard him say to his kindred,
  In the course of a friendly chat,
"These men think they are above us,
  Yet they drink such stuff as that!
Oh, the poor degraded creatures!
  I am glad I am only a bird!"
Then he flew up over the meadow,
  And that was all I heard.

PIPING ROBIN

By Annette Wynne

PIPING Robin, piping so.
Tell the snow
It's time to go;
Tell the rough winds not to blow
Any more through field and glen ;
Call the bluebirds home again,
Tell the little flowers to grow,
Piping Robin, piping so!

SOMETIMES

By Annette Wynne

SOMETIMES I think I'd like to be
Small as a robin in a tree.
So I could be with little things
That go on tiny feet or wings.

But other times I'd like to be
Tall as the robin's very tree,
So I could stretch out very far
And be with great big things that are.

SPRING

By Annette Wynne

THE robin saw the new spring bonnet
On a small maid's head,
And called the seeds to look upon it,
In the flower bed;
Soon there was a growing sound,
The flowers peeped up all around,
And all the birds began to sing—
And it was spring!

BIBLIOGRAPHY

THE PETITION OF THE RED-BREAST
BY WILLIAM ROSCOE,
    First published in *Mount Pleasant: A Descriptive*
    Poem - to which is Added, an Ode, 1777
EPITAPH ON A FREE BUT TAME REDBREAST
BY WILLIAM COWPER,
    Written in March 1792. Published in *Works, Comprising*
    his Poems, Correspondence, and Translations. With a Life of
    the Author by the Editor, Robert Southey, Volume X, 1837
INVITATION TO THE REDBREAST
BY WILLIAM COWPER,
    Written in March 1792. Published in *Works, Comprising*
    his Poems, Correspondence, and Translations. With a Life of
    the Author by the Editor, Robert Southey, Volume X, 1837
THE REDBREAST CHASING THE BUTTERFLY
BY WILLIAM WORDSWORTH,
    Written on 18th April 1802 and first
    published in *Poems of the Fancy,* 1807
AN EPITAPH ON A ROBIN REDBEAST
BY SAMUEL ROGERS,
    First published in *Poems,* 1816
ROBIN REDBREAST BY GEORGE WASHINGTON DOANE,
    First published in *Songs by the Way Chiefly Devotional,*
    with Translations and Imitations, 1824
TO THE ROBIN BY CHARLES TENNYSON TURNER,
    First published under the title "XXVII. To a
    Redbreast" in *Sonnets and Fugitive Pieces,* 1830

THE REDBREAST
(SUGGESTED IN A WESTMORELAND COTTAGE)
BY WILLIAM WORDSWORTH,
    Written in 1834. First published in *Poems*
    Founded on the Affections, 1835
THE AUTUMN ROBIN BY JOHN CLARE,
    First published in *The Rural Muse*, 1835
THE WOOD ROBIN BY WILLIAM THOMPSON BACON,
    First published in *Poems*, 1839
TO A ROBIN BY HANNAH FLAGG GOULD,
    First published in *Poems, Volume II,* 1839
THE ROBIN'S HYMN BY HANNAH FLAGG GOULD,
    First published in *Poems, Volume II,* 1839
THE ROBIN BY JONES VERY,
    Published in *Essays and Poems*, 1839
TO A REDBREAST BY WILLIAM WORDSWORTH,
    First published in *Miscellaneous Poems*, 1842
TO ROBIN REDBREAST BY GEORGE MEREDITH,
    First published in *Poems, Written in Early Youth*, 1851
ROBIN REDBREAST BY WILLIAM ALLINGHAM,
    First published in *Fifty Modern Poems*, 1865
HOW THE ROBIN CAME
BY JOHN GREENLEAF WHITTIER,
    First published in *Snow-Bound*, 1866
ROBIN REDBREAST'S REWARD
BY JAMES RYDER RANDALL,
    First published in *The Pacificator*, unknown date.
    Republished in *The Southern Poems of the War, Collected*
    and Arranged by Emily Virginia Mason, 1867
THE ENGLISH ROBIN BY HARRISON WEIR,
    Written in 1858. Published in *The Poetry of Nature*, 1868
THE ROBIN BY JOHN GREENLEAF WHITTIER,
    First published in *The Pennsylvania Pilgrim*, 1872

THE ROBIN'S NEST BY PHOEBE CARY,
   Published in *Ballads for Little Folk by Alice and Phoebe
   Cary, Compiled and Edited by Mary Clemmer Ames,* 1873
THE GOLDEN-ROBIN'S NEST
BY JOHN WHITE CHADWICK,
   Written in July 1874. First published
   in *A Book of Poems,* 1875
A NEW VERSION OF WHY
THE RED ROBIN'S BREAST IS RED
BY PAUL HAMILTON HAYNE,
   First published in *Poems of Paul Hamilton Hayne,* 1882
BLEAK WEATHER BY ELLA WHEELER WILCOX,
   First published in *Poems of Passion,* 1883
TAMPA ROBINS BY SIDNEY LANIER,
   Written in 1877. First published in *Poems
   of Sidney Lanier, Edited by his Wife, with a
   Memorial by William Hayes Ward,* 1884
THE ROBIN REDBREAST BY MATHILDE BLIND,
   First published in *The Ascent of Man,* 1889
ROBIN'S SECRET BY KATHARINE LEE BATES,
   First published in *Sunshine, and Other
   Verses for Children,* 1890
IF I CAN STOP ONE HEART FROM BREAKING
BY EMILY DICKINSON,
   First published under the title "VI." in *Poems by Emily
   Dickinson, First Series, Edited by her Two Friends
   Mabel Loomis Todd and T. W. Higginson,* 1890
MAY-FLOWER BY EMILY DICKINSON,
   First published under the title "II." in *Poems by Emily
   Dickinson, First Series, Edited by her Two Friends
   Mabel Loomis Todd and T. W. Higginson,* 1890
IF I SHOULDN'T BE ALIVE BY EMILY DICKINSON,
   First published under the title "XXXVII" in *Poems by
   Emily Dickinson, First Series, Edited by her Two Friends
   Mabel Loomis Todd and T. W. Higginson,* 1890

THE ROBINS' OTHER NAME
BY JAMES WHITCOMB RILEY,
  Published in *Rhymes of Childhood*, 1890
A WINTRY SONNET BY CHRISTINA ROSSETTI,
  Published in *Poems*, 1890
THE ROBIN BY EMILY DICKINSON,
  First published under the title "VI. The Robin" in *Poems
  by Emily Dickinson, Second Series, Edited by her Two
  Friends Mabel Loomis Todd and T. W. Higginson,* 1891
ROBIN'S MISTAKE BY ELLA WHEELER WILCOX,
  First published in *How Salvator Won,
  and Other Recitations*, 1891
THE ROBIN IN JANUARY
BY HENRY CHARLES BEECHING,
  First published in *Love's Looking Glass*, 1892
THE ROBIN'S FAREWELL BY CLARA DOTY BATES,
  First published in *From Heart's Content*, 1892
ROBIN BY JOHN BANISTER TABB,
  First published in *Poems*, 1894
TO A WOOD-ROBIN BY JOHN BANISTER TABB,
  First Published in *Poems,* 1894
HOW DARE THE ROBINS SING BY EMILY DICKINSON,
  First published under the title "XII" in *Poems by Emily
  Dickinson, Third Series, Edited by her Two Friends
  Mabel Loomis Todd and T. W. Higginson,* 1896
COMPARISON BY PAUL LAURENCE DUNBAR,
  First published in *Majors and Minors*, 1896
TO THE WOOD-ROBIN BY JOHN BANISTER TABB,
  First published in *Lyrics,* 1897
OWL AGAINST ROBIN BY SIDNEY LANIER,
  Published in *Poems of Sidney Lanierm,
  Edited by his Wife*, 1899
TO THE FIRST ROBIN BY RAY CLARKE ROSE,
  First published in *At the Sign of the Ginger
  Jar; Some Verses Gay and Grave*, 1901

ROBIN REDBREAST BY JOHN BANISTER TABB,
First published in *Later Poems,* 1902
ON A REDBREAST SINGING AT THE
GRAVE OF PLATO (IN THE GROVE OF ACADEME)
BY WILLIAM SHARP,
First published in *The London Academy, March* 11th 1904
TO THE OREGON ROBIN BY JOHN BURROUGHS,
First published in *Far and Near,* 1904
WHY ROBIN'S BREAST IS RED BY JAMES R. RANDALL,
First published in *Maryland, My*
Maryland, and Other Poems, 1908
FLOWER AND THORN BY THOMAS BAILEY ALDRICH,
Published in *Early Poems,* 1908
THE ROBIN BY DORA SIGERSON SHORTER,
First published in *The troubadour, and Other Poems,* 1910
ROBIN'S MATE BY ELLA GILBERT IVES,
First published in *The Evolution of a Teacher,* 1915
ROBIN REDBREAST BY WILLIAM HENRY DAVIES,
Published in *Collected Poems,* 1916
THE ROBIN BY THOMAS HARDY,
First published in *Moments of Vision,* 1917
HOME BY FRANCIS LEDWIDGE,
First published in *Last Songs,* 1918
A SPRINGTIME WISH BY ISABEL ECCLESTONE MACKAY,
First published in *The Shining Ship, and*
Other Verse for Children, 1918
PIPING ROBIN BY ANNETTE WYNNE,
First published in *For Days and Days: A Year*
Round Treasury of Child Verse, 1919
SOMETIMES BY ANNETTE WYNNE,
First published in *For Days and Days: A Year*
Round Treasury of Child Verse, 1919
SPRING, by ANNETTE WYNNE
First published in *For Days and Days: A Year*
Round Treasury of Child Verse, 1919

Printed in Great Britain
by Amazon

54410866R00096